ICEBREAKER

Seventh Edition

Seventh Edition

A Manual for Public Speaking

Tracey L. Smith
Lewis and Clark Community College

Mary Tague-Busler
Lewis and Clark Community College

WAVELAND
PRESS, INC.
Long Grove, Illinois

For information about this book, contact:

Waveland Press, Inc.
4180 IL Route 83, Suite 101
Long Grove, IL 60047-9580
(847)634-0081
info@waveland.com
www.waveland.com

Cover and unit-opener graphics: Niki Busler

To our daughters,
Ashley, Jessica, Nicole, and Kelsey.

You are our inspiration.
We know you have had to live and breathe communication
your whole lives, but we think it was well worth it.
You are successful students, mothers, workers,
women, and people.
We are so proud of all of you!

Contents

Preface

This edition of *Icebreaker* has a distinctive and unique format. We have organized the text into seven units. Each unit covers one or more elements of the nine-step speech process we have used in earlier editions. However, this edition details each step more specifically, and the ordering of the units follows the organizational pattern of actually creating a speech. We begin each unit with a series of questions that act as a framework to stimulate the reader's interest and to preview what's ahead. We answer the questions within the unit. We have also retained the "Strengthen Your Skills" exercises within the text so that readers can practice essential elements of public speaking. We have found that the down-to-earth "question/answer" approach to covering important concepts, together with Strengthen Your Skills exercises, helps readers gain a deeper understanding and gain confidence as they learn. We have eliminated the appendixes but have moved that material into the appropriate units in which the information is discussed.

Changes incorporated into this seventh edition have evolved from our own combined experience in using the text in both higher education classes and business training sessions. We have also included information based on comments and suggestions from our colleagues and users of the previous edition. We are very excited about this new edition!

We would like to thank our families, colleagues, and friends for their patience and understanding during this time-consuming process of revising the text. We also thank our students and readers for their suggestions that have been incorporated into these revisions. We hope this seventh edition of *Icebreaker* provides you with a clear and comprehensive overview of the speech process that you can use to hone and enhance your public speaking skills.

To the instructors who have assigned *Icebreaker* throughout its multiple editions—Thank you for your continued support of this text!

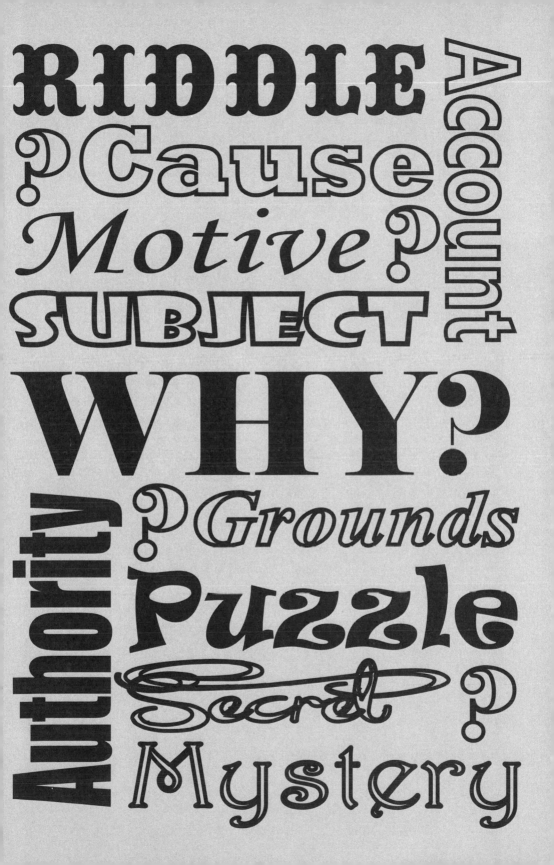

Why?

. . . we need to be able to exchange thoughts and ideas . . .

- Why Is Communication Important?
- Why Do We Need to Study Speech Communication?
- Why Is Communication a Process?
- Why Use Nine Steps to Prepare a Speech?
- Why Do Speakers Make Mistakes?

Life is full of questions. You are probably asking yourself questions about the study of public speaking right now. Most people attempt to understand any new process, idea, or situation by formulating a list of questions. As they begin to find answers to these questions, they will begin to feel more comfortable with the new concept. We will approach the study of public speaking in the same way. Public speaking is a new experience for many people, and no doubt you will have many questions as we begin our study of it. We have started this first unit with words that represent the word "why." *Why* do I need to study public speaking? *Why* do I have to take this class? *Why* is it required at my college? *Why* do I need skill in public speaking?

In this unit we provide information that will answer these questions for you and help you begin to lose some of the anxieties you may have about public speaking. This text is divided into seven units. Each unit covers a basic universal question; who, what, when, where, why, and how. In this unit we will cover *why* we study communication, and we introduce you to a nine-step process that will help you prepare a speech from beginning to end.

We often take our communication for granted, not realizing how important communication is in our daily lives. Communicating with others on a daily basis requires the ability to exchange our thoughts, feelings, and ideas. To function effectively in society, you must be able to get your messages across to all kinds of people in many different types of situations. How do you explain your project to your boss at work? How can you get the mechanic to understand what that funny noise is in your car? How do you get your kids to clean their rooms? How do you ask for the help you need from a friend? These are only a few instances where good communication skills are important and essential.

Why Is Communication Important?

Some of the skills you have used in everyday conversations are similar to those you will learn for public speaking. The skills you learn in this class will help you in your personal, professional, and civic lives. Although you may not think you will ever give a speech in "real life," you will, and you have been involved in many situations every day that require you to share important information with others through speech.

Oral communication has been used throughout history in many cultures. These societies believed that the ability to speak effectively in public was critical to the success of their respective way of life. The ancient Greeks and Romans believed that effective oration, the ability to speak well in public, was crucial to their political and educational framework. Over the centuries there have been many men and women who have shared their visions of the world from the podium. Some of these notable speakers are John Quincy Adams, Abraham Lincoln, Elizabeth Cady Stanton, Dale Carnegie, Martin Luther King Jr., Nelson Mandela, Steve Jobs, and Princess Diana. Public speaking is an important means for sharing information. It can help people increase their feelings of individual self-worth, enhance their professional life, and help them participate in government.

The types of speeches you are asked to deliver in a modern-day public speaking class haven't changed much in almost 6,000 years! There is a long history of public speaking in all societies and a well-tested understanding of why speaking effectively is important. While it is impossible to pinpoint the date, speaker, or topic of the first speech delivered, we can safely state it predates any written form of communication. Literacy, especially widespread public literacy, is a very recent development in human history. It was the spoken word that spread and preserved information in the past.

All societies, tribes, and nations had storytellers whose job was to pass on history and culture. These were honored and respected roles, and were found in ancient India, Africa, China, among the Aztecs, in North and South America, and throughout Europe. Speaking has always been important to people. In fact, *The Precepts of Kagemni and Ptah-hotep* (3200–2800 BCE) stresses the importance of public speaking and even gives guidelines for effective communication that are still used today! This document is the oldest book of the Egyptian kingdom and devotes much of its text to the discussion of oral communication, or public speaking. Early Greek, Roman, and medieval cultures devoted much time and study to "rhetoric," which is the theory and practice of public oral communication.

Republics that practice democracy, like the United States, can trace their roots to early Greek society. Early Greek society functioned within a framework similar to our modern-day democracy. Citizens gathered to receive new "information," whether it was about a new state holiday or a change in taxes. Since handbills, phones, and the Internet weren't available, any public communication was handled orally during these gatherings. Therefore, good citizenship required attending functions in the public forum, and citizens were deemed worthy based on the public speaking skills they displayed there.

There were times when citizens were called on to debate or vote on a governmental issue. This required citizens to be able to convince others to agree with them; in other words, the art of persuasion was necessary. Finally, citizens were expected to attend special occasions and events held in the town square, once-in-a-lifetime occurrences that required special attention. These early Greek traditions of (1) speaking to inform, (2) speaking to persuade, and (3) speaking for special occasions provide us with the framework for modern-day public speaking. In the United States, teachers of communication still devote considerable effort helping students learn methods that support the use of effective communication techniques within these three categories.

In the United States, we live in a democratic society that allows freedom of speech. Therefore, we, too, have a responsibility as members of our society to participate in our republic. As individuals living in a democracy, we can freely communicate our ideas to one another. This is accomplished by sharing your ideas and opinions through the skill of public speaking. It is one way we can learn to be critical thinkers and listeners. The authors of the Constitution knew the importance of citizen participation and educated decision making. They provided a framework for a democracy unlike any other in the world. It is our responsibility to continue to make it work. What you learn from a course in public speaking can make you a better citizen and a skilled, functioning member of our society. Hence, the goal of a public speaking course is to provide you with the opportunity to learn skills necessary to achieve success in all aspects of your life, including your civic responsibilities.

Presenting speeches will depend on your audience. Explaining the effects of tanning to an audience of high school seniors is different from presenting your opinion about how your church committee's budget should be spent to an audience of the members of your church, and this is very different from giving a toast at your best friend's wedding. In the first example, you would be providing facts and *information* to your audience. In the second example, you are attempting to get your audience to share your viewpoint through the art of *persuasion*. The final example requires you to speak to your audience at an event designed to celebrate a uniquely *special occasion*. These three examples also represent the three types of speeches in public speaking and we owe their basis to the speaking platforms of the early Greeks.

Communication requires the efficient and effective exchange of ideas and feelings between and among people. Public speaking is based on the same principles. It doesn't matter whether you are deciding what activity to do this weekend with friends, or if you are in a board meeting presenting an explanation of your financial report; getting your ideas and viewpoints across to another person or persons requires the same skills for both situations.

Perhaps an analogy will help clarify this message. Speaking to a group of friends versus speaking to an assembled work group is analogous to the similarities and differences between writing a personal email and writing a business email. For both types of correspondence, your goal is to share information. The differences occur only in the specific form that the email takes. In an informal email to a friend you might not be concerned with sentence structure, spelling, or punctuation. You might refer to examples without explaining them or use slang terms that you and your friend share. In a business email you would be very concerned with the grammar, spelling, and punctuation. You would also be sure to use words properly and in their correct form and structure, while avoiding "text speak." An informal discussion with friends versus a formal speech or discussion is very similar to this example. Essentially the difference is one of form, not purpose. Consequently, the skills you learn in a public speaking class can easily be transferred to your daily communication interactions, resulting in fewer misunderstandings and clearer messages being delivered.

Why Do We Need to Study Communication?

We have already discussed the importance of communication in our lives. However, many of you may still not be convinced that the skills you learn in a public speaking class will ever be used again once you complete the course. The goal of communication is to relay your ideas in a way that is understandable to others. When you attempt to communicate, you want the other person(s) to understand what you are saying. While there are some obvious differences between being the keynote speaker at a company's annual conference and talking to your five-year-old son, the general purpose is *exactly the same*! As the keynote speaker, your goal is for one-thousand audience members to comprehend your message. As a parent, your goal is for "one" son to understand your directions. The audiences and messages are different, but the purpose is the same, to achieve understanding. Therefore, we need to study communication, and learn how to become effective speakers in order to achieve these important outcomes in our lives.

The skills necessary to deliver a speech can be used to tutor your child or help a sibling with her homework. They can help you successfully talk a friend through a problem or provide instructions on home improvement. Think about your everyday conversations. Wouldn't you like to be able to present your viewpoint in a way that others would consider valuable? Need to convince your children that they should clean their rooms, or your parents to extend your curfew? The principles you will learn in this speaking course are exactly what you need to make these day-to-day communication situations successful. Hopefully you are beginning to see the need to study communication, and that being an effective speaker in any situation simply means adapting your speaking skills to individual situations. At the conclusion of this course, you should be a more effective speaker both publicly and privately.

So far we have examined the importance of communication and why we need to study it in general. It is now time to take a look at the process, or what is happening when we actually communicate in a public or private situation.

Why Is Communication a Process?

Before you can learn to speak more effectively in any communication situation, understanding the elements of communication is necessary. **Communication** is the process of thinking and feeling, receiving and conveying messages to ourselves and others in a manner that brings ideas and people together. The communication process is best understood by using a simple model. A **model** is a simplified representation that is used to understand a more complex device, process, or concept. The diagram below illustrates the communication process and shows areas where it can become confusing or less effective. Being aware of these areas will help you, as a **communicator,** deliver and receive messages more effectively. To illustrate this process, we will use a model that attempts to freeze a split second in the communication process so we can see what is happening.

Experiences have happened to us from the day we were born. These experiences are stored in our memory and play a role in shaping how we think and feel. These experiences create who we are and how we view the world. In communication we call these collective experiences our

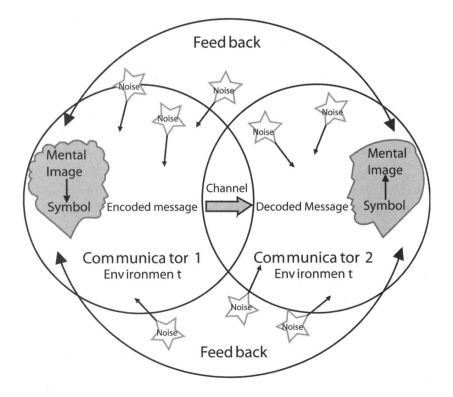

personal environment. In order to communicate effectively with someone else, we must isolate those experiences we want to convey to others to help us form a message that another person can understand.

The first step in sending a message occurs when a person (communicator 1) has an idea, opinion, or feeling and wants to let another person (communicator 2) know about it. When we experience a thought, we do not initially think about it in words, but experience it as a mental image or **symbol.** For example, let's say you want to ask someone to see a movie with you Friday night. The beginning of this idea occurs with your mind "seeing" you and your friend at the theater. The process of turning a mental image into a symbol is called **encoding.** Once you have completed this encoding process you have a message to send to another person. The **message** is the symbol or idea you want the other person to understand. Your encoded message must travel through some medium or **channel.** The channel may be **verbal elements,** which refer to spoken or written language, and/or **nonverbal elements,** such as posture, facial expressions, eye contact, or even the tone we use when we say our words.

Once the encoded message travels through its channel, it arrives at its destination, communicator 2. This is the person whom you want to understand what you are attempting to communicate. Since communication consists of sending and receiving messages, listening is another essential component in the process. **Listening** is the psychological process of understanding the message after the physical process of **hearing** has occurred. Communicator 2 must hear the message and make a conscious psychological effort to turn the message back into a mental image. The process of turning a message that has been received back into a mental image, or symbol, is called **decoding.** This process is the same whether you are speaking to one or several people. Therefore, the model can be representative of a conversation between two people or a speaker delivering a speech to an audience of 50 people. While this may appear to be a linear process (the message starting at point 1 and ending at point, 2), communication is really a simultaneous process. This is because both communicators are sending their messages back and forth to each other at the same time. In our example, communicator 2 is probably watching communicator 1 while she is asking him to go to a movie. The fact that he is using eye contact, a form of nonverbal communication, while she is speaking makes his message occur simultaneously to hers. This constant exchange of messages results in what is called **feedback.** Feedback can be verbal or nonverbal and is what makes communication a two-way simultaneous process.

Many times the message sent (encoded) is not the message received (decoded). For example, let's say you (communicator 1) want to describe a square to another person. You choose the words to send your message, but when communicator 2 decodes the message, his or her mental image is of a rectangle, not a square. Why did this happen? Obviously the message sent was not the message received. By looking at what actually causes ineffective communication, we can lessen the likelihood of the message being misunderstood.

1. ***The encoded message was unclear.*** The first reason that a message is misunderstood is because the encoded message was unclear. When you do not clearly encode your message, the other person cannot understand what you mean. There are many reasons why a message may not be clearly encoded. We might leave out important information in our verbal communication. This means that the words chosen to represent our mental images were not detailed enough to be understood by the receiver of the message. Maybe, as I'm leaving for school, I ask you to take the trash out today. When I come home the trash is still in the house. I am angry because you did not do as I asked. You don't understand why I'm angry; it is only 7:00 PM and there is still a lot of time "today" to take out the trash. My omission of a specific time to take out the trash in an encoded message caused you to misunderstand the message after you decoded it. Another reason a message might be unclear is if the receiver misinterpreted the nonverbal communication in my encoded message. For example, I might choose to use a gesture to communicate. I raise one finger causing you to think I want one piece of bread, but I am really gesturing for you to wait a moment while I decide. Effective communication requires a complete and clear message to be developed in the encoding process before it is sent, verbally or nonverbally. Otherwise, it is likely that miscommunication may occur.

2. ***The sender and receiver do not share the same personal environment.*** The second cause of messages going astray is that the communicators may not share the same personal environment. Personal environment includes everything that has been experienced by a person: education, religion, home atmosphere, historical background, moods, and so on (represented in the diagram as circles around the communicators). No two people share exactly the same personal environment. We are all individuals who are unique in many

ways, although our personal environments can and often do overlap in certain areas. The shared parts of our environments can help us understand each other better. When our environments differ in an area we are trying to communicate about, very often communication becomes ineffective. As an example, suppose the sender is awake and happy, while the receiver is tired and grouchy. The sender says, "Gee, you look attractive today," meaning it as a genuine compliment. The receiver, because of his or her different mood (personal environment), interprets this message as an insult and replies, "I suppose you mean I don't look good any other day!" The message sent wasn't the message received, and miscommunication has occurred due to the different experiences, or personal environments, of the two communicators.

3. *The receiver was distracted by noise.* The final cause of miscommunication is noise interfering with a person receiving a message. **Noise** is any distraction that hinders communication. Arrows on the model represent the interference of noise. There are two general types of noise: external noise and internal noise. **External noise** can be audible sounds produced outside your ears—factory machinery in operation, people talking on their cell phones, children arguing, televisions blaring, or other people talking—that make it difficult to concentrate. External noise can also include nonaudible interferences such as a hot room, an unpleasant odor, an uncomfortable chair, or a text message. External noise hinders our ability to hear or listen to what is being said. This may cause us to misinterpret all or part of the message being sent.

Internal noise is caused by the thoughts and feelings we are experiencing inside our minds or bodies. When your mind is already preoccupied with daydreaming or worrying about an exam, you are experiencing internal noise. Internal noise can also be caused by actual hearing problems or defects. A person who is hearing impaired—either permanently or temporarily, as from a bad cold—may find it difficult to understand a verbal message.

Any, all, or a combination of what causes ineffective communication may result in the message sent not being the message received. Being aware of how communication occurs and knowing where possible problems might arise will help you be a more effective speaker. This is true whether you are speaking to a friend, your family, your coworkers, or your public speaking class.

Strengthen Your Skills

Make Your Own Model

Purpose: The purpose of this exercise is to help you identify those areas where the message sent may go astray.

Procedure:
1. Collect magazines, scissors, paste, and markers, or use your favorite drawing app.
2. Create your own communication model.
3. Clearly label areas where communication goes astray.
4. Explain your model to your classmates to give you practice speaking to an audience.

We often take our communication for granted. Considering how important it is in our lives, this can be a problem. We've all experienced situations where we were misunderstood, and the message we thought we sent was not interpreted in the manner we intended. Investing time and energy to learn how to be effective communicators will keep this from happening as often, resulting in more effective communication interactions with the various people in our lives.

Now that we have explored communication in general, let's look specifically at public speaking. Many beginning public speaking students believe that preparing a speech is the same as writing a research paper. This is not true! The steps required for preparing material that will be delivered orally differ from those that you might use if you were writing a paper. Although each begins with choosing a topic, the rest of the process differs significantly. A paper usually is not read aloud and therefore isn't affected by the author's verbal and nonverbal delivery. Organization, tone, and audience appeal is made in writing not orally. The majority of a writer's time is spent in correcting, editing and rewriting the document.

A speech also requires preparation. In fact, we tell our students that about 95 percent of the work they will do to present a speech is in the preparation process. However there is an obvious difference between a paper and a speech. Speeches require an oral presentation that must also be prepared in advance and practiced. This requires a different approach than the one you are familiar with from English class. If you are used to writing term papers, the steps we will cover for speech preparation may seem somewhat awkward at first. Nevertheless, once you begin to use them, you will find that they are necessary and effective in helping you adapt your communication skills to those that will work when you need to deliver an organized and professional speech at the podium.

Why Use Nine Steps to Prepare a Speech?

Before we begin to look at each aspect of preparing an effective speech, it is useful to look at an overview of the **speech process.** This process incorporates and summarizes the concepts, skills, and practices that will be discussed in greater detail in later units of this book. Even though we look at these areas separately, they all work together. Seeing the whole picture prior to investigating its individual parts is often a helpful tool in the learning process. This list can also be used as a checklist when you are working on an actual speech assignment. Throughout the rest of the text, we will refer to this list as the nine-step speech process.

The Nine-Step Speech Process

1. *Select a general topic.* Pick a **general topic** based on personal interest. Assuming you haven't been given a topic by your boss (or instructor), pick a topic that interests you. Getting your audience's attention is much easier to do if you already have an interest in the subject about which you are speaking. Next, you must narrow your topic. For example, your general speech topic may be dogs. However there are probably hundreds of things you could discuss about dogs. You must *narrow,* or adjust, your topic to your interests, those of the audience, and the overall purpose of the speech. Failing to give consideration to all three items will decrease your effectiveness.

2. *Focus your topic.* We have learned that the first step to presenting a great speech is to choose a topic and then narrow that topic by considering your own interests, those of the audience and the occasion or event at which you will be speaking. Once you have narrowed your topic you must **focus** that topic to appeal to the specific audience to which you will be giving the speech. This process is known as *audience analysis* and is an important part of preparing a speech. This occurs in step 2 and can be accomplished with the use of a working plan for your speech. This *working plan*

will define your audience and incorporate what you learn about them into the speech occasion, and the speaking environment.

3. *Consider your specific purpose.*   Consider why you are being asked to present the speech. Is it to inform your audience, to persuade them to take some action, or to mark some special occasion? Looking at the objective you have in mind (or have been assigned) will help you to form a **specific purpose,** and help your audience arrive at your expected result.

4. *Organize your speech.*   How you **organize** your speech saves you time when you research your topic, as you will only need to find information for the specific main points you will cover in your speech.

5. *Research your topic.*   Please note that this is step 5 of the process, not step 2! Don't move from selecting your topic to finding information for your speech. You need to focus your topic so you will know what type of information you need to find; otherwise you will waste time wading through material that does not fit your needs. Remember that there are many sources of information, and you want to use the most current and credible material you can find to support your main points.

6. *Create* **presentation aids.**   Beginning public speakers tend to ignore one of the most obvious ways to make a speech more effective. Elements that *show* the audience what you are describing, allow them to *hear* something, or in some other way help them *experience* your words will add to the effectiveness of your speech. Charts, graphs, pictures, and PowerPoints can be used as well as video recordings. YouTube clips, iTunes, and other Internet resources are all ways of adding dimension and interest to your speech.

7. *Create speech notes.*   This step is very important and is often ignored by students preparing speeches. Once all of your information has been gathered and you have developed aids for your speech, it is a good idea to create some type of device that will aid you when delivering your speech to your audience. Many beginning public speakers try to memorize or read their speeches. These are not the best ways to deliver a speech. It is important to have your thoughts written as bullet points in case you forget an idea or stumble during your speech. Creating these notes in advance also gives you the opportunity to use them to practice your speech.

8. *Practice.*   Practice makes perfect, right? Well, maybe not perfect, but close. Your goal is to present an effective speech, and *practice* can help you attain this goal. One of the main benefits of practicing is that it helps you become familiar with what you will say and how you will say it before you actually present your speech to an audience.

9. *Deliver your speech.* Many of you will say that this step is the one that you are the most anxious about. If you have completed the other eight steps, much of your work is already done. This step occurs when you stand in front of the audience and orally present your ideas. This is actually the step that requires the least amount of time!

In addition to knowing what steps are necessary for delivering an effective speech, it may be useful for you to know why mistakes are made by speakers. These mistakes often result in confusion in your audience and in an ineffective speech. There are seven mistakes often made by beginning speakers. Examining these mistakes in detail can help you to avoid them while preparing your own speeches.

Why Do Speakers Make Mistakes?

1. They try to cover too much information.
2. They fail to focus the speech for the specific audience.
3. They don't properly organize the speech.
4. They forget to state sources orally during the speech.
5. They fail to use notes and presentation aids to help illustrate ideas.
6. They avoid the use of gestures and eye contact while speaking.
7. They ignore time constraints.

Obviously, making sure that you have completed all nine steps of the speech preparation process will help you avoid these common mistakes. Although we will cover these issues in more depth in the next few units, a few words about each item will give you an idea of why these mistakes should be avoided and help emphasize why the nine-step process is so effective in preparing a speech.

The first mistake is to choose a topic that is too broad or doesn't interest you. Anything can be a speech topic, but it is important to realize that you can't tell everything to everyone. Keep in mind you will have to adjust your choice based on your audience (step 1).

The second mistake is failing to focus your speech for a specific audience. If you have decided that your speech is to inform your audience about the type of pet that would best suit their lifestyle, then you must ask questions of your audience to help you determine what that lifestyle actually is. You may need to ask them if they live in the city or the country. You may ask them if they live in an apartment or a house. You may need to know how much time they can devote to the care and training of the pet they choose. By using the information you gain from questioning your audience, step 2 of the process, you can focus your research, and ultimately your speech, to this *specific* audience. If your speech is about dog ownership, you will be able to tell them that for people who live in high-rise apartments, where outdoor areas are not easily accessible, it's best to own smaller dogs, because they don't require a large amount of outdoor exercise and therefore can be left indoors for long periods of time. Or you might be able to tell your audience which pets (in general) are best suited to individuals who live in a house with a yard. By specifically tailoring your information to the audience, you can avoid the mistake and be on your way to formulating a specific purpose statement, step 3 of the process.

The third mistake made by beginning speakers is that they don't organize their information. Even if your speech is focused for a specific audience, you may still have gathered too much information during the research process. When researching, it is important to carefully consider whether each piece of new information is necessary for a particular audience by creating an effective organizational pattern, step 4 of the process. By doing so you will be keeping in mind your main points and can decide if the information you have found supports one of those ideas. If not, do not use it, no matter how interesting you think it may be! Keep in mind that most speeches have time limits, so you must relay the most important information you find while researching in the time allotted. Keeping these restraints in mind can help you to avoid making this mistake as well.

The fourth mistake made by beginning speakers is that they do not attribute their sources in their speeches. In step 5 you have completed the research for your speech. We will cover how this is done in the research unit. For now, keep in mind that you must give credit where credit is due. For example, if you have taken weeks to prepare your speech and deliver it, and then your teacher awards your A to someone else, how would you feel? Not very happy, we imagine! The same is true for other authors or researchers. They have put tremendous effort into researching their areas of expertise. When using their ideas to help support one of your own, give them credit. Stating in your speech that your information comes from particular sources is easy to do and makes your audience feel comfortable about believing what you have to say can be trusted. You can easily add these sources as part of your speech notes.

The fifth mistake made by many speakers is one that we tell our students should be avoided at all costs. In fact, we usually require our students to use notes and at least one presentation aid for each speech that they deliver. Notes keep a speaker on track and able to relay all of the information necessary as well as serve as a reminder to orally state the source of the information being conveyed. You can also mark when you want to use your presentation aid within these same notes. The reason for presentation aids is that most people do not learn new information by hearing it alone. People assimilate new information best through visual means, or by seeing something that relates to the information being presented, steps 6 and 7 of the process.

The sixth mistake usually occurs because speakers are nervous when they are delivering their speech. This makes them afraid to look at their audience or use their hands. Keep in mind that most face-to-face communication occurs when people are looking at each other. This is true whether the communication is occurring between you and your boss, or you and a large audience. It is also important to use your hands and face because they add interest while you are speaking. This occurs naturally in most communication interactions. Your audience will expect you to point if you are giving directions, or smile if your information is humorous. If you fail to use gestures and facial expressions at the appropriate time during your speech, your audience will be confused. Gestures, facial expressions, and eye contact are necessary and important components in all communication, and public speaking should be no different. You can incorporate these elements during practice, step 8 of the speech process.

The seventh and final mistake to avoid, as a beginning public speaker, is that of ignoring the time limit that has been set for giving your speech. If the dinner is supposed to be served at 7:00 and you have been scheduled to speak for 15 minutes beginning at 6:30, then you are expected to wrap up 15 minutes before dinner. This would give you time to return to your seat, as well as give the wait staff time to move about the room and deliver the meals to those in attendance. If you ignore this and speak for 40 minutes, dinner is interrupted. Your audience is likely to become irritated and stop listening to you. Your goal as a speaker is to make sure your audience gets your intended message. They can't do that if they are hungry or otherwise mentally occupied. Again, practicing your speech, step 8, can help you adhere to your time limit when you actually deliver the speech, step 9, the final step of the speech process.

Strengthen Your Skills

Critique Your Instructor

Purpose: Here's your chance to turn the tables on one of your instructors by "grading" his or her lecture. By critiquing someone else's presentation you can more easily see what you may be leaving out of your own future speeches.

Procedure:
1. Pick one of your instructors and critique his or her lecture one day in class.

2. Refer to the seven common mistakes above and note any made by your instructor.

3. Make note of how effective his or her lecture was and why or why not.

Conclusion

We often take our communication for granted. Considering how important it is in our lives, this can be a problem. We've all experienced situations when we were misunderstood—the message we thought we sent was not interpreted in the manner we intended. Investing time and energy to learn how to be effective communicators will prove to be advantageous in our personal and professional lives. We discussed why we need to communicate and how learning skills for public speaking can be adapted to our daily lives. We have discussed why communication is a process and why it is necessary to use a step-by-step process to create a speech to ensure that we don't make any of the common mistakes made by speakers.

Now that you've been introduced to the speech-making process, it's time to begin looking at how you can complete each individual step for preparing an effective speech. We know from our experience and research that audiences are more inclined to pay attention to a speech if they can realize some advantage in doing so. If you pay attention to the importance of communication, and to the nine steps for preparing a speech, you can ensure that you avoid making any of the seven mistakes that speakers make, and ensure that your speech has personal meaning for your audience.

■ DISCUSSION QUESTIONS

1. What historical evidence is there that speaking effectively is an important skill valued by all cultures?
2. How are speaking to your family and speaking to a larger audience the same? In what ways are they different?
3. What causes messages to go astray? Give an example from your own life that illustrates how this can be avoided in the future.
4. What do you think is your biggest problem when communicating with others? What are your strong points?
5. Why is each of the "nine preparation steps" essential?

■ KEY WORDS

channel
communication
communicator
decoding
encoding
external noise
feedback
focus
general topic
hearing
internal noise
listening

message
model
noise
nonverbal elements
organize
personal environment
presentation aids
specific purpose
speech process
symbol
verbal elements

FUNDAMENTAL

? Matter

Theme? Idea

CONTENT

WHAT?

? PURPOSE

Topic Subject?

Consideration

What?

... select a general topic ...
... step 1 ...

- What Do I Know?
- What Don't I Know?
- What Can I Do To Find a Topic?
- What Do I Do Once I Choose One?
- What Is The Three-Step Narrowing Process?

The first step to presenting a great speech is to choose a topic. What will you speak about? While this should be the easiest and least time-consuming of all the steps you will take to prepare a speech, novice speakers often find this a difficult and time-consuming task.

The first thing to consider when choosing a topic is you! What do you know that might be interesting to someone else? Experiences have happened to you in the past and continue to happen to you every day: Fascinating, funny, frightening events occur that could make excellent topics for speeches. You may believe that you are a boring person, to whom nothing ever happens. This is just not true! You could talk about a recent problem you had in school, a family crisis you are facing, a new hobby, or your job. Any of these subjects would make a very good speech. Additionally, these topics are all about you, a subject that most audiences will find fascinating. Humans are very curious creatures and generally enjoy finding out about other humans. Your audience members will enjoy comparing their experiences to your own. When we share personal information in this fashion, we are placing ourselves in a larger context, tying our experiences to those of our audience. Through this sharing of experiences, we become connected personally to our listeners.

How can I, Mary, turn my altercation with the manager of a local discount store into a speech? I might talk about the rude clerks and employees we have all encountered. I might speak about the pressure the employee faces when having to deal with an irate customer for whom he is totally unprepared. I might discuss, in involved and humorous detail, how I tried to return a defective bedspread to the store. I insisted I had purchased it there; only to find out I had purchased it at the discount store down the street. The store name was printed right on the receipt! This speech does not have to be looked up or researched, it really happened to me! But with a little research effort I could easily add to the content by discussing various store return policies and procedures, therefore creating a detailed informative speech about that topic. What else do you know that could become a speech topic?

What Do I Know?

The easiest starting place for generating a **speech topic** is to stop for a moment and think about everything that you personally know. What are some hobbies you have? What sports did you play in high school? What are you currently involved in outside the classroom? Do you have any particular interests or concerns about your life or your health? Do you find your job interesting, fulfilling, or time-consuming? What is your experience with college? Let's explore these ideas further with some examples.

Suppose you are concerned that you may have exposed yourself to the risk of skin cancer because of how much time you are spending outside in the sun. After all, you have heard the warnings about skin cancer. You know that exposure to the sun at an early age can cause problems later in life. After talking with your doctor, you now wear sunscreen if you are in the sun for prolonged periods, and you also wear a hat when you go fishing. As you continue to explore this experience, you must keep in mind that your audience is composed of people who probably have shared a similar experience. This is to your advantage because it allows you to speak to them about something they can easily relate to. However, you don't want to bore them with information that they might already possess. Finding some detail or fact they might not be aware of is important. For example, you might mention that leather is derived from exposing skin to intense chemical heating processes. Not a pretty picture when applied to our own skin! You could explain what to look for in sun protection products. You could explain the concept of ultraviolet light, harmful rays, and SPF. The goal here is to start with something familiar that your audience can grasp and then expand that subject to include information that is unique. In fact, linking new ideas to those already known by your audience is a very effective technique.

What Don't I Know?

To find "unique" information about a subject, you must be willing to explore and be honest with yourself about what you don't know. Although you have some previous individual experience with various subjects (a good starting point), there are details and points about each you probably don't know that could be added to your knowledge. For example, most of us have read and studied the Declaration of Independence. Most people know it was written in Philadelphia. What you might not know is it was written during the hottest summer on record! How would you behave if you had to sit in a stuffy, un-air-conditioned hall, in the elaborate and hot clothing of the day, with people who bathed once a week at best, debating the future of your nation? This tidbit, added to your speech on the perseverance of our forefathers in creating and preserving democracy in America, might be just the unique information you need to keep your audience interested.

You must be willing to research the possibilities of everything you don't know to make your speech interesting! Research is also important to make sure facts are substantiated. You will be spending a lot of time with your topic, so pick something you are really interested in. Don't choose a topic just because you think you can easily find the research material.

Beginning with a topic that interests *you*, even if you don't know everything about the subject, will make your research more exciting as you find out all the unusual facts about it. Your research will be easier and more efficient if you have interest in your subject, and you will be motivated to stick to your topic. When possible, *pick a topic you are interested in!* If you are still having trouble choosing a topic, there are many other ways to find one. The following section discusses what to do to generate more speech topic ideas.

What Can I Do to Find a Topic?

Brainstorming

One easy technique for generating speech topics involves writing down ideas "off the top of your head." This process is called **brainstorming.** The best way to brainstorm is to quickly list ideas as they occur to you, until you collect many ideas. Problem-solving groups in corporations often use this method when they are looking for solutions to unusual problems or addressing challenging concerns. The key to brainstorming is to suspend judgment about any single idea while ideas are being generated.

An example of how a company solved a problem associated with a smoke-free workplace illustrates the brainstorming process (and also provides a good, potential speech topic!). Since laws about smoking have been initiated in the State of Illinois, smoking is prohibited throughout the entire workplace and within 15 feet of the entrance, exit, or ventilation intake of a workplace. Yet, Illinois law doesn't address the specific areas of a workplace where smoking may be permitted. Therefore, a large discount store has a no-smoking policy within 15 feet of all entrances to the building. However, employees began to hang out in large groups just beyond the prohibited area to smoke during their breaks. Customers complained about walking through the smoke, and many stated that they felt it looked very unprofessional. Reports showed that customers believed they would not be able to get help inside the store because all of the employees were outside smoking! Therefore, customers were choosing to shop elsewhere. Regardless of whether these customers' perceptions were true, the store now had a "perceived" problem.

To find a solution to this problem, the store had to suspend all judgment until a large number of possibilities to solve it were generated. They formed a committee of people to find a solution to the problem. It did not matter whether the committee members were smokers or non-smokers. The key was to list as many possible solutions as they could. Some suggestions included: banning smoking on company property, hiring only nonsmokers, no breaks, no lunch, and so forth. As you can see, brainstorming does not always produce feasible (or legal) solutions! However, the company eventually came up with the plan of providing a large outdoor seating area, furnished nicely with tables, chairs, flowers, and ashtrays. Employees were happy, and customers perceived the company as wonderful and caring for giving its employees such a pleasant break area. As an added bonus, the customers no longer perceived the employees as unprofessional or unavailable. So, generating a list of possible solutions and then choosing the best one for an individual situation solved a "perceived" problem.

Another technique to aid you in the brainstorming process is to use **hitchhiking.** Hitchhiking is the process of building off of other topics/subjects you have already listed. Suppose as you are brainstorming you write down "fast food." That might trigger several related topics such as

McDonald's, Burger King, Pizza Hut, pizza, hamburgers, and so forth. This creative technique is called hitchhiking.

Strengthen Your Skills

Brainstorm Topics

Purpose: The purpose of this exercise is to take you through the process of choosing possible topics for speeches by brainstorming.

Procedure:

1. Your instructor will divide the class into small groups of four or five.

2. Each group should appoint a record keeper.

3. For 10 minutes, group members will throw out possible topics while the record keeper writes them down. Keep the following rules in mind:

   a. Simply list ideas, don't judge them.
   b. Hitchhike off other ideas. If one person says "music," add ideas that stem off that, like "rock," "hip-hop," "alternative," "country," etc.
   c. Remember that your purpose is to compile as many topics as you can.

4. At the end of 10 minutes, stop and review your topics. Could any of these be of interest to you as a speech topic?

General Conversation

Another excellent method for generating topics is **general conversation.** There are several times throughout any given day that you will find your-self sitting with friends and acquaintances having a conversation. You may be waiting for a class to begin or chatting over lunch at McDonald's. You might be on your computer, tablet, or smartphone and receive a text or a message from someone on Facebook. You share opinions and concerns while you communicate with others. Someone may be concerned about his or her grades; another may be having financial difficulties, while you may be worried about getting the flu! Each of these seemingly minor subjects could produce a speech topic. For example, concerns about grades could lead to a speech on how to study, various testing methods, course selection, course requirements, financial aid, choosing a college, deciding on a career, and so on. These ideas, although started in general conversation, can be brainstormed or hitchhiked into an enormous list of possible speech topics!

Other Sources

Our daily routine can also provide us with speech topics. Your local newspaper and various magazines that you read offer a wealth of useful, interesting, and most importantly, current information. Your browser home page usually includes headlines and stories of interest. These are often the best sources for up-to-date facts on issues. Television programs can also offer you many ideas. There are several learning channels, animal-oriented stations, and reality adventure series, among many others, that can give you interesting facts to begin or support your speech. Digital recording makes it simple to record these potential sources for later use. Also, don't forget you! Your personal daily routine can provide you with a viable speech topic. We take much of our daily routine for granted. For example, brushing our teeth is something most of us do at least once per day. This topic alone can provide several speech topics: good oral hygiene, tooth decay, gum disease, and implants, to name a few! These are topics oriented to your own life and can be easily shared with your audience. In addition, familiar quotations or sayings can serve as good topics for icebreaker speeches. On the following page is a "Strengthen Your Skills" exercise using this idea.

The Internet

Finally, don't forget the Internet. Just one page of a single site will provide you with a multitude of possible topics. Even those annoying pop-up ads can have a use for *you* rather than the advertiser. Another idea is to use your favorite search engine to search general topics. The result should give you lots of ideas without even linking to the sources. For example, a search for *television* will result in thousands of possible topics, from a biography of your favorite celebrity to television's effect on our culture. Don't get bogged down, pick a single topic and get started!

What Do I Do Once I Choose One?

Once you've decided on a general topic for your speech, it's time to narrow that topic—the process of fine-tuning your topic to reflect

Strengthen Your Skills

The One-Proposition Speech

Purpose: This exercise gives you practice in applying one central idea to your personal life. You will create a short speech that explains one proposition and illustrates it in a variety of ways.

Procedure:

1. Choose one of the following parables as your speech topic:
    *   Don't cry over spilt milk.
    *   The grass is always greener on the other side of the fence.
    *   If at first you don't succeed, try, try again.
    *   A stitch in time saves nine.
    *   An ounce of prevention is worth a pound of cure.
    *   Early to bed, early to rise, makes a man healthy, wealthy, and wise.
    *   Blood is thicker than water.
    *   A penny saved is a penny earned.
    *   Walk softly and carry a big stick.
    *   No man is an island.
    *   If the shoe fits, wear it.
    *   Man does not live by bread alone.
    *   The die is cast.
    *   The early bird catches the worm.
    *   Beauty is only skin deep.
    *   Nice guys finish last.
    *   No news is good news.
    *   It's not if you win or lose, but how you play the game.
    *   It's not over 'til it's over.
2. Tell your audience what the statement means to you in your own words. Try to avoid the actual statement if possible. Use illustrations and examples from your personal life to enhance your speech.

what effect it will have on your audience. If you want to be a successful speaker, you need to learn how to properly narrow your speech. This is one of the most important elements of an effective speech, but it's also one of the steps beginning speakers fail to do thoroughly. Remember that the time and effort you put into this simple process will decrease the amount of time you spend on research later and lead to a much better speech in the end.

What Is the Three-Step Narrowing Process?

A successful speaker uses his or her own interests as a factor in selecting a topic and delivering a speech and then considers how the audience may react to that topic, while also thinking about the occasion for which he or she is giving the speech in the first place. This three-step process can help you to effectively narrow your speech so that the time you need to spend on research later is significantly reduced.

Consider the Speaker

The first step in **narrowing** considers you, the speaker. Ask yourself these questions:

- What *interests* me about this topic?
- What is the *reason* for this speech?
- What *knowledge* do I have about this topic?

Interest

A successful speaker always uses his or her own *interests* to help decide what message will be sent. Even if the topic is assigned in some way, like a business report you've been asked to prepare, it will be much more effective if you show enthusiasm and enjoyment for the topic.

Let's suppose you have chosen the author Anne Rice as your general topic. In this part of the process you should narrow that topic so that it reflects a clearer statement of why Anne Rice is interesting to you. Will you talk about her books or her personal life? If you decide it's her books, which genre will it be—vampires, witches, her erotic works, or her series on Christ? Which do you *personally* find most interesting?

Reason

Next you must consider the *reason* you are presenting the speech. Do you want to persuade your audience to read a series of her books? Do you want to inform them about her history of depression, or her return to religion after decades of being an atheist? What purpose will this speech fulfill? One way to determine this is to make a list of objectives. For the Anne Rice speech this list may include learning about the Vampire Lestat, reading all the various vampire books, or believing that personal adversities can be overcome. At this stage you may have several ideas, and that's fine.

Knowledge

The last step is to consider what *knowledge* you have about your topic. Even though you are interested in the topic, there are probably some areas that you have more knowledge about than others. Your speech should be about what you know. You'll most likely need to enhance the information you already have by doing research, but having a good basic knowledge of your topic not only gives you a starting point, it also means you'll spend less time doing research. Using the Anne Rice example once more, if you know little about her personal life but have read all the vampire books, your best choice is to go with the books!

At the end of this process you will have a better idea of what your topic will be. In fact, you probably will have several possible speech topics. The next step will whittle down all these possibilities by considering the most important element, your audience.

Consider the Audience

You may think you are speaking because of requirements from your boss or your teacher. You may think you are giving a speech for a grade or to follow orders. While these are certainly common elements of some speaking situations, seeing them as your main purpose won't result in an effective speech. Many of us might think we would prefer not to have an audience for our speech because it would decrease our anxiety—but what purpose would that really serve? A speech requires a speaker *and* an audience. You are only one part of the equation. Your audience is the other part of that equation. You need to *consider* them, too, when narrowing your topic. Finding the answers to these questions can help:

- How can I make this topic of *interest* to my audience?
- What is my audience's *reason* for listening to this topic?
- What does my audience already *know* about my topic?

Interest

This part of the narrowing process relies heavily on getting to know your audience. A topic that is of no *interest* to your audience will result in a doomed speech. You need to make sure your speech topic is interesting to them. In order to do this, you will have to consider your audience's interests, and much more. Just as you needed to know what made your topic interesting to you, you need to know the same thing about your audience.

You can't cover everything; so you need to choose carefully based on those interests you and your audience share. Remember you are talking to a *specific* group of people. You may be able to use the same general topic for different groups, but it must be individually tailored to the specific interests of each group. Even after beginning speakers narrow a topic for themselves, they often believe that what they are interested in will bore others. How can you gain and maintain attention? What interests do you and your audience share in regard to your topic? Consider the following true example of how you might approach this problem.

Mark was enrolled in a public speaking class. There were 3 men and 15 women in the class, which met on Monday nights during the fall semester. Mark loved football and wanted to do his informative speech on some aspect of that topic. However he was well aware that the majority of the class were women who may not be interested in football. While he bemoaned the fact that he was missing the televised games on Monday nights because of class, he had heard many of the women saying they were glad to attend class and let the men in their homes have the TV on Monday evenings. How in the world would he narrow this topic so that it was of interest to all of his audience and himself? There was a solution, and it worked beautifully! Mark decided to do his speech on the hand signals the officials use to call a play. Instead of just explaining them in the context of a football game, he took the interests of his audience into account. He described a couple out on a first date. Every time the guy made a move that corresponded to a hand signal (like fumbling, unnecessary roughness, or touchdown), he had a female member of the class demonstrate the signal in his speech. His audience paid attention, enjoyed themselves, and learned more about football from his speech.

Reason

Not only do you have to consider your audience's interest in your topic, you also need to make sure your topic relates to the *reason* your audience has gathered. What is their purpose for listening? Why should these people listen to *you*? What will they learn or be able to do at the end of your speech? What needs will your speech fulfill? Will they have a new easy-to-make recipe, have a better understanding of how the stock market affects them, or be better informed voters? Will they save money, be healthier, or be safer in their homes?

Discovering your audience's reasons for being present helps you focus your speech. For example, you would probably assume that most of your classmates are enrolled in this class to fulfill a requirement for graduation, with the greater goal being a degree, certification, or promotion at work. While that would be a fairly accurate assumption, what other reasons could they have? Are they there to socialize, or get out of the house while the kids are at school? Are they there to prove to someone that they are intelligent? Finding out other possible reasons may help you relate your speech topic to your audience's real reason for listening to you. Incorporating these reasons in your speech can help your audience achieve the result you want for them at the end of your speech.

Knowledge

The audience's *knowledge* level should also be considered when narrowing your speech topic. While some people may politely sit and listen to a speech about something they already know, this is the exception rather than the rule. Most will tune out and quit listening, and as mentioned before, a speaker without an audience can't deliver an effective speech. You need to know what they know. Is their knowledge basic or does a significant part of your audience have advanced knowledge about your topic? Giving a speech on the basics is good if your audience knows very little (or has misconceptions) about a topic. Giving this same speech to a group that already knows the basics won't work. You want to provide your audience with new information, unique data, and new ways of thinking about your topic. You probably won't have an audience in which all members have the same level of knowledge. You'll have to aim for middle ground, without ignoring the lower and upper knowledge levels of the audience.

Adapting your topic to a specific audience is probably the most important part of the narrowing process.

Consider the Occasion

Once you've considered the speaker and the audience, the last part of this three-step process considers the **occasion** for which you are speaking. To understand the speaking occasion, ask yourself the following questions:

- What *event* marks my speech?
- What is the *physical environment* of the speech location?
- What is the *time factor* for my speech?

Supplying answers to the above questions will complete the narrowing process and prepare you for the next step in developing an effective speech.

Event

What is the *event* for which you are preparing your speech? Does the event mark a wedding, athletic banquet, or business meeting? While the same topic may be used in several different situations, the topic may need to be modified depending on the event at which you will speak. Your topic would be completely different for a speech given at a church function than for a speech at the local Harley club. If your topic was persuading people to vote for a particular candidate, you might focus on the candidate's values or morals when speaking at a church function. In your speech to the Harley club, you might emphasize your candidate's stance on helmet laws, highway safety, and tax advantages for nonprofit organizations. You might use humor in both speeches but change the amount and type used. You might choose different language or words for the church group as compared to the motorcycle club. Think about the event and make sure you adjust your topic appropriately.

Physical Environment

Knowing the *physical environment* of the occasion in which you will be speaking and what equipment you will have available to you is also important. If you are speaking in a fifteen-hundred–seat auditorium, you will need different equipment than if you were speaking in a boardroom. Will you need a microphone to be heard? Do you have the equipment available to deliver a multimedia presentation, or will handouts be necessary? Will the audience members be close enough to you to see small photographs, or will they have to be scanned and projected onto a large screen? These are just some of the factors you need to consider about the physical location where you are speaking.

Time Factor

The last step when considering the speech occasion is the *time factor*. You've considered the event and the physical environment for the occasion you will be speaking at, but will your topic fit within your allotted time? In many ways, this last step is the most difficult. All speeches have time limits. Time limits are important. Former President Bill Clinton is an experienced speaker and is considered by many people to be very effective. He can enchant his audience. However, he was never able to speak in the allotted time frame. Traditionally, in the State of the Union Speech, the president speaks about an hour to Congress. President Clinton's speeches typically lasted two hours. He could not stay on topic, often rambling and deviating from his script. Since his speech did not stay within the expected and allotted time frame, he was less effective with Congress and the American people watching him on TV. Know what your parameters are and stay within them. Failure to plan for the time limit can have unpleasant results.

Trying to cover too many points in your speech, or not covering enough, can leave the audience feeling confused or cheated. Further, if there are other events planned in addition to your speech, a speech that takes more than or less than the allotted time can interfere with the schedule. Let's say you have been asked to speak for 30 minutes and your speech is an hour. Whatever follows your speech, be it another speaker, dinner, or the audience's dismissal to do other things, is disrupted if your speech runs past the allotted time. Know what your time limit is and make sure your speech fits within your time frame.

Strengthen Your Skills

Narrowing Your Topic

Purpose: The purpose of this activity is to give you practice in how to narrow a topic.

Procedure:

1. Make a list of five general topics that consider you as the speaker. Choose topics you are interested in, you know something about, and would either inform or persuade your audience.

2. Now consider your audience. This could be your classmates, people you work with, or members of an organization. It doesn't matter what group you pick, just make sure you have a specific audience in mind. For each of the topics you listed in number 1, decide what changes need to be made to make it interesting to your chosen audience by considering their knowledge and reason for listening.

3. Now consider an event, physical environment, and time factor (say 5–7 minutes) for each topic.

This three-step narrowing process is an important part of preparing an effective speech. It is a necessary process to achieve your goals. No step should be skipped. The result of completing this process will allow you to create a plan that takes into consideration you, your audience, and the occasion so you will be further able to adapt your topic to your audience. The next step in the process is known as focusing which we will cover in the next unit.

Conclusion

Remember that the sooner you pick a topic for your speech, the less anxiety you will feel. Make sure to narrow your topic so that it "fits" all the criteria. This is an important three-step process that you shouldn't skip. When you consider the desired result you want from your audience, it helps you to create a speech that will interest your audience. This may seem trivial and may seem unimportant to the novice speaker, but it is actually an essential part of an effective speech. Giving an effective speech requires much more than just telling the audience something. It demands that the speaker form a bond with the audience—that's what narrowing your speech can help you do.

■ DISCUSSION QUESTIONS

1. List several methods of generating ideas for speech topics.
2. Should you evaluate topics during brainstorming? Why or why not?
3. How does "hitchhiking" help generate topics?
4. What is narrowing, and why is it essential to creating an effective speech?
5. Why is adhering to a time limit important?
6. You have narrowed your topic for yourself as the speaker. You find it interesting, are knowledgeable about it, and it suits the reason you are speaking—to inform. Can you assume that it will "work" for your audience? Why or why not?

■ KEY WORDS

brainstorming   occasion
general conversation   speech topic
hitchhiking

PEOPLE

? They We ?

HIM He

WHO?

MEMBERS

Persons ? Them

She & Her

Who?

... focus your topic ...
... consider your specific purpose ...
... step 2 and step 3 ...

- Who Is My Audience?
- Who Is Listening?
- Who Is Having Trouble Listening?
- Who Has Poor Listening Habits?
- Who Will Understand My Speech?
- Who Is Experiencing Speech Anxiety?
- Who Can Overcome Speech Anxiety?

We have learned that the first step to presenting a great speech is to choose a topic and then narrow that topic by considering your own interests, those of the audience, and the specific occasion or event at which you will be speaking. Once you have narrowed your topic you must then **focus** that topic to appeal to the specific audience to which you will be giving the speech. This process is known as audience analysis. It occurs in step 2 of the nine-step speech process and can be accomplished with the use of a working plan for your speech. This **working plan** will define your audience and incorporate what you learn about them into the speech. Careful attention to all of the elements in a working plan will make your job as speaker much easier.

Who Is My Audience?

Let's examine each of the three elements of a working plan more closely and determine how each element helps you to determine who your audience is so that you can adjust your speech to their needs.

People: Element One

If you want to keep your audience members' attention while you are speaking, it is important to know as much information about them as possible. You must first determine who the people are in your audience. What do they know? What do they believe? What are their personal characteristics, habits, or lifestyles? These questions can be answered by conducting a survey, called an **audience analysis** that contains questions that help you to learn more about your audience. Audience analysis is a common method used throughout the retail goods industry to find out about consumer preferences. For example, have you ever made a purchase and been asked to provide your zip code to the clerk at checkout as part of a survey being conducted by the store? Knowing their customers' zip codes is a way for that store to gather information that can help determine the income levels and perhaps the lifestyles of the consumers who are shopping there. This information might help in product placement or in determining what products to carry, so the store can cater to its customers. The audience analysis you complete for your speech is similar. You will ask your audience questions that will help you determine how to tailor your topic specifically to their needs and wants.

It is important to note that audiences can be both individual and collective. Often your group will respond as a whole (as when they are all college students). Sometimes they will respond as individuals (some are dental students, others history majors, etc.). This is often the case when psychological issues, such as morals and lifestyle, are surveyed. Here is an exercise to help you analyze your classroom audience.

In order to further understand your audience members, you must consider their **needs** and desires in the initial stages of your speech. Basically, human beings have two types of needs: physical and psychological. **Physical needs** include food, clothing, and shelter. A speaker who suggests a program of buying groceries more economically, lowering fuel bills, or providing a more efficient smoke detector could probably gain immediate audience attention. He or she is speaking about basic needs that all members of the audience can relate to and share.

Psychological needs can be far more difficult to identify, but, as human beings, there are some psychological needs we all share: Friends and loved ones are important to most people, as is the need to be a contributing member of society. We also have individual goals and desires. While the complex personality of each member of the

Strengthen Your Skills

Audience Analysis

Purpose: To learn how to analyze an audience.

Procedure:

1. Your instructor will divide the class into groups of five to seven. Group members should discuss their individual characteristics: age, income, religion, educational level, lifestyles, morals, etc.

2. The groups should have approximately 20 to 30 minutes for discussion.

3. After discussions, pool the information for the entire class and analyze the results.

4. The results should show the overall characteristics of your classmates, therefore providing you with an "analysis" of your audience for this class.

audience cannot be known and may seem to present a challenge too large in scope for any speaker, you can likely identify and address the needs of the group as a whole.

Asking your audience questions will help you to gather: **demographic data**—measurable statistics such as age, gender, occupation, education, and income level—about your listeners as well as **psychological data**—measurable information about such characteristics as attitudes, morals, values, religious beliefs, and lifestyle. The information you gain will help you understand your audience better so that you can speak directly to them. It will help you gain their interest by speaking about things that relate to their specific personal beliefs, experiences, knowledge, and lifestyle. For example, if you were giving a speech about saving money for retirement, the demographic and psychological data collected from a group of college students would be vastly different than that of a senior citizens' group! Gathering this type of information will help you to decide what to put in your speech that will be interesting to the people present. The results you receive from your questions can be related specifically to your topic and used in your speech. This information will help you to eliminate or add information as you do research and further prepare your speech.

Making assumptions can be dangerous, so avoid making any about your audience. Find out as much about your audience and their characteristics and beliefs as possible. Informative and special occasion speeches benefit from asking questions one and two. Persuasive speeches require you to also ask questions three and four.

1. *What do your audience members already know about your topic?* This will help you decide how much research you need to do on your topic.

2. *Where did your audience get its information?* Is the audience's information credible? Is it biased? Is what they know based on their opinion or is it based in fact.

3. *What is your audience's position on your topic?* You need to know if audience members' thoughts and opinions are extremely strong, average, or apathetic, especially for a persuasive speech. Not only do you need to know how they feel about your topic, you need to know the intensity of their convictions. It's one thing if I believe that Habitat for Humanity is a good organization that I would support with a five-dollar donation. It's a much stronger level of involvement if I spend every Saturday for four months helping to build a house. This will help you direct the development of your speech.

4. *What's the audience's emotional reaction to your position?* Are their feelings logical and based in fact? Are there contradictions you can use? For example, if you ask Tracey if she supports a woman's right to choose abortion, she will reply, "Yes, it should remain law." On the other hand, if you ask her how she feels when she thinks about abortion, she will reply, "Sick and sad." It's important to know both reactions if you are going to persuade your audience to adopt your stance, and it can be equally important when giving an informative speech because it can help to guide your research.

Once you have completed your fact gathering, you must apply these facts to help you focus your speech. Of course, *audience* is a collective term and within that audience you will have differences. The key to a successful speech is to attempt to reach out to as many members as you can.

Now that you have done your first audience analysis of the members of your class, remember that you need to do this same process for any audience you may be asked to speak to, in or out of the classroom. By going through this process, you have prepared for the first element in your working plan, *the audience*. Next, you must apply the information you have learned about your audience to the speaking occasion at which your audience is present. The audience members present will share a reason for attendance. Knowing the occasion, and why people are present, can give you valuable information about who your audience members are.

Occasion: Element Two

The **occasion** for which you are speaking refers to the actual event requiring a speech. This event could be a company's annual conference, a student senate meeting, a classroom presentation about a topic being studied by students, or a report to the budget committee. Knowing why you and your audience are gathering will help you set the direction your speech should take and is the second element of your working plan. It is also important to know how much time has been allotted for your speech, and how much time is required for you to make all of your points. If you are asked to speak for 10 minutes, your audience will expect you to speak that length of time, not less or more. Think about meetings at work. Typically you will know how long to speak in such a situation from previous meetings. What happens if someone speaks longer? That's right, people tune out and start thinking about all the work they need to get back to or what they want for lunch. Time is often one of the most frustrating elements in your plan, because you must be organized enough to cover the material without exceeding the time allotted.

Once you have adequately determined why you are meeting and have planned for the length of your speech, you will have information about your audience as well. A company meeting consists of company employees; a classroom of psychology students would be studying psychology concepts. Knowing the occasion helps you know more about who your audience is. You have now completed the second element in your working plan. You are now ready to plan for the speaking environment. Although this may not seem like it will help you know who your audience is, it does in a roundabout fashion. If your audience is gathered in an auditorium, they will all be exposed to sounds that may echo, or distance interfering with their ability to hear. If you know the physical environment, you can adjust for these issues and adapt your speech to help your audience overcome these issues.

Speaking Environment: Element Three

The **speaking environment** is the third and final element of the working plan. The environment you will be speaking in consists of the facility and general area in which you will address your audience. Will you be speaking in a classroom, in an intimate living room, at a conference table, or in a large auditorium? Will there be a podium, a microphone, a digital projector? What if you are demonstrating how to paint holiday ornaments? Are the necessary supplies, including water, accessible? Will the audience members be able to see you from their seats? Will you have access to the Internet? Knowing where you will speak and what equipment will be available to you is the third and final element in your working plan. Knowing this information makes the process for creating a working plan for your speech important even if your instinct is to stop at narrowing your topic. The process is very similar to the narrowing process we learned in step 1 of the speech process so it may seem redundant. However, a working plan takes narrowing a step further by adding detailed and specific information about your audience so you can know "who" they really are! The only exception now is: planning for the unexpected!

Although your goal as a speaker is to be so well prepared that nothing will go wrong, anyone who has ever planned anything knows that if something can go wrong, it will. The important thing to remember is through your working plan you have further considered the three basic elements that will always be present during a speech: the audience, the occasion, and the environment. Knowing this information in advance can help you make adjustments if they become necessary on the actual day of your speech. The process of giving a speech is quite complex. It requires more planning than just throwing some ideas on note cards and jumping to the podium. In order to make a success of public speaking, the speaker must consider many circumstantial factors. The working plan builds on the narrowing process and focuses your topic to be the beginning format for the detailed speech preparation to come. It is these basic elements that are providing you the opportunity to speak! Unexpected events can cause nervousness and speech anxiety, but if they occur, they can be handled smoothly if you have a well-devised plan.

Now that we have found out detailed information about who our audience members are and have created a working plan that incorporates this information into the occasion and event for our speech, we must think about how we can keep our audience interested in our topic. It is a good idea in this unit to think about the listening process and how our audience will or will not be attentive to our speech.

Who Is Listening?

The most important job a member of the audience can perform is that of being an attentive listener. Listening is a skill that is very important and yet all too often taken for granted. We assume that if we hear something, we have listened. This is not always true. Hearing is just the first step to listening. It occurs when the reverberation of sound waves in the ear causes a signal to be sent to the brain. In other words, it is the physical aspect of listening. Just because we *hear* something doesn't mean we *listen* to it; in fact, we hear a large number of things in any given day to which we don't actually listen.

There is more involved in listening than sound waves. In fact listening is a psychological process that involves five steps. Hearing is just the first step in the process. The other four steps are attending, evaluating, retaining, and responding. All five steps must be completed in order for the listening process to have truly occurred. Let's examine what happens at each step so that we can determine ways in which we can become a better audience member.

1. **Hearing** is the first step in the listening process. In this step, sound waves from the atmosphere around us reverberate in our eardrums and send signals to the brain. Our brains receive the signals and begin the process of trying to interpret the audible stimuli. Unless you suffer from hearing loss or some other impairment, this step occurs unconsciously.

2. **Attending** is the second step in the listening process and consists of us trying to pay attention to the sounds we are hearing. We must make a conscious effort to direct our thoughts to the sounds being experienced. In the case of being an audience member, you must pay

attention to the words the speaker is using and attempt to understand their meaning.

3. **Evaluating** is the third step in the listening process. In this step we must try to evaluate the speaker's message and attempt to understand what he or she is trying to communicate to us. We will determine if the information is important to us, whether or not it is familiar, or if it matches some prior experience or knowledge that we may have. We often make judgments about a speaker and his or her message in this step, and we sometimes reject or accept the speaker's ideas based on this evaluative process.

4. **Retaining** the information occurs in this step. This is often one of the most difficult steps in the process. We must rely on memory to help us recall information over a short time span in order to help us continue to understand the information being relayed by the speaker.

5. **Responding** is the final step in the process. If we have been able to complete all four of the preceding steps, then we will provide a response to the speaker that indicates that we have received his or her message. This is the step that constitutes an indication to the speaker that we have attempted to evaluate the message. This is the step that we also know as "feedback," from our study of the communication model in unit 1.

Now that we have examined the five-step listening process, it is important to realize that the process occurs sequentially. If any of the steps are omitted, listening has not occurred. There are many things that can cause a step to be omitted and skipped. It is these things that distract us and can cause us to be poor listeners and inattentive audience members. You may fool some people into thinking you are listening when you're not, but you won't gain the information that you may need from the conversation or presentation. Although statistics show that for most of the day, people are in situations in which they should listen, only a few people actually do. There is very little risk involved in listening, and the benefits far outweigh the cost of the time spent listening. If listening is so important, why don't we do it more effectively? As a speaker, how can we get our audience to listen to our speech?

Who Is Having Trouble Listening?

Most of our communication interactions in any given day are one on one, rather than as an audience member listening to a speaker. However, regardless of the type of interaction in which we are participating, we are often distracted by external elements. When these distractions interfere with one of the steps in the listening process, they can cause the entire process to breakdown. Unfortunately it is human nature to not pay attention to information that does not interest or motivate us. Most people need some sensory stimulus to engage them in the listening process.

Research suggests that many of us have one sense we primarily use to assimilate information. This **sensory mode** is how we comprehend new information. For most of us this primary sense is sight. We rely on visual cues to help us make sense of new information. Some people rely on auditory cues, or the things they hear, to digest data, and we all occasionally use our senses of touch, smell, and taste to increase our knowledge. What would happen if you, as the speaker, relied strictly on your voice and the words you were speaking to gain the attention of the audience? Would most of your audience pay closer attention to you if they could "see" what you are talking about? The answer is yes.

While audiences usually respond to their favorite subjects, or information concerning them personally, how can you incorporate everyone's personal sensory mode and individual interests into one speech? Speakers must be very clever to construct their message so the audience, as a whole, can relate to the message. The audience's responsibility is to find something in the speaker's message that is personally motivating or interesting. If we can learn how to find that mutual key, we will tend to speak and listen with much more concentration. The problem is that most people have a problem finding something that motivates them to listen, and then have more problems staying focused on the speaker when concentrating for any length of time. When this happens regularly over time, we begin to display behavior that keeps us from listening.

Who Has Poor Listening Habits?

We tend to give in to the distractions around us causing us to display behaviors that indicate we are not listening. In fact, we have a series of slogans that describe these nonlistening behaviors, such as "giving someone the cold shoulder" or "staring off into space." The fact that most people speak at the rate of only 200–250 words per minute, while our brains are capable of processing at least twice that number or more, leaves time for our minds to wander.

We give in to distractions so often that it becomes a habit. **Habits** by definition are any behaviors that we engage in consistently and unconsciously over time. Because of these habits, honing your listening skills can be a difficult process since awareness is the first step in change. Habits are behaviors in which we engage automatically and repeatedly. Therefore, we do them without even thinking about them. Tuning out is one of these automatic behaviors. We are so used to being overloaded with information that we shut down. The first step to overcoming this poor habit and becoming an effective listener is to realize when we are not paying attention and are tuning out. We can then make a conscious effort to get back on track and pay attention.

Antilistening behaviors result when we give in to distractions. Sometimes we display these behaviors because we do not have any formal training in listening. Some of us are even taught not to listen, primarily through observing how often others tune us out. Just think of all the times you are asked to spend listening in just one day. You listen to teachers, to bosses, to friends, and to family. Because we tend to confuse listening with hearing, we regard listening as a passive activity. We expect it to occur because we have two ears! This expectation causes most of us to be terrible listeners. Although we may have received instruction over the years about how to speak, we very seldom receive any instruction on how to listen. If we have any past training in listening, it was probably focused on antilistening behaviors. For example, Mom says, "We don't listen to that kind of language." Your friend Jane says something hurtful to you and your sister tells you, "Oh, don't pay any attention to her." We are frequently told not to pay attention to what people say. This is not the best method for sharpening your listening skills!

We are exposed to many messages on a daily basis. We must make decisions as to which information needs our attention. These various bits of information often overload us with messages. This concept, known as **message overload,** is a significant factor in poor listening. We are in situations that require us to listen during most of our waking hours. Our ears and mind are bombarded with messages from people throughout the day. We are expected to listen to friends, family, coworkers, bosses, instructors, and numerous other individuals. We can become distracted by the numerous messages we receive. When we reach a saturation point in attempting to listen to everything, we often simply tune out. We may do this so often that it becomes a habit, resulting in poor or ineffective communication. Let's discuss some other things that may distract us in the listening process.

We often make **assumptions** about what a speaker might be saying. This, too, can cause us to fail to listen. We may decide that we don't have to listen to what is being said, for many reasons. We may believe that we have heard the information before, that we already know what the speaker is going to say, that the message is insignificant, or that the information is of no concern to us. Sometimes we think that what the speaker is saying is too complicated for us to understand, and we would be wasting our time paying attention to the message. We frequently let our perceptions about a speaker's appearance or personality influence our decision to listen. We may not like what the speaker is wearing, or the tone or pitch of the speaker's voice. Although these perceptions may seem unfair, it is often human nature to judge others critically. Sometimes we may fear that the information the speaker is presenting will cause us to feel bad or require us to make a decision. These assumptions divert our attention from the message before we even really know what the speaker is trying to say. We will tune the speaker out, engaging in anti-listening behavior once again.

Sometimes we are distracted by noise. We introduced this concept in unit 1 as any distraction that interferes with the communication process. Audience members may be **preoccupied** with other thoughts. This *internal noise* is caused by your own thoughts, your **intrapersonal communication.** Maybe you are worrying about an exam you have to take later in the day, or you are not sure whether you got the job you interviewed for yesterday. When we are preoccupied with our own thoughts, we cannot listen to others. We will often choose, or select, which part of a message we want to listen to and tune everything else out. Most of us are so busy in any given day that we display this habit on a regular basis.

Studies have found that improving your listening skills not only increases effective communication but also provides many other benefits—such as better grades, better relationships, improved work environments, and increased family harmony. For purposes of this class, sharpening your listening skills can help you to be a better audience member. In order to become a better listener it is important to determine what distractions you are likely to give in to and how you can break this cycle.

If you have recognized any of your own behaviors in the preceding information then you have taken the first step toward understanding how difficult it may be to be an audience member or for your audience to pay attention and listen to your speech. If you understand why you tune out, then you can take steps to avoid having your audience tune out, helping them to become more attentive audience members during your speech.

Improving Your Listening Skill

Remember, listening is a skill. Most skills can be learned and practiced. If you want to improve your listening skill and become a more effective listener, especially when you have to listen to a speech, then the following four suggestions will help you achieve your goal.

1. ***Don't expect the speaker to entertain you.***   Frequently we believe that it is the speaker's responsibility to make us listen. We think that if the speaker cannot keep our interest, then we don't need to listen. Effective speakers attempt to keep their audiences interested, but that doesn't mean we, as listeners, don't have responsibilities as well. We must mentally prepare to listen to the speaker. Tell yourself that you can stay focused because you want to understand what is being said to you.

2. ***Use the speaker's speaking rate to your advantage.***   We think faster than most people can speak and this is one reason we may fail to listen. But this can also help us to listen as well. Use the extra time to think about the speaker's words. Review what has been said or take notes to keep yourself on track.

3. ***Listen to the message, without the bias.***   We often fail to listen because something we see or know about the speaker turns us off. However, information can be learned from speakers whose images or agendas don't match our expectations, ideas, or opinions. Judge the content of the message, not the speaker, and withhold evaluation until you've listened to the whole message.

4. ***Get rid of distractions.***   Clear your mind. Put away papers and books that may distract you from listening. Turn off radios, TVs, iPods, phones, or other distracting electronic devices. Try to concentrate on the speaker instead of on your own thoughts. Try not to react emotionally to the message. Filter out noise and focus on the speaker.

In a public speaking situation you have a responsibility to listen when you are part of the audience. You will be providing feedback that will help the speaker judge the impact his or her speech is having on you. As a speaker you will need to learn how to "listen" to this feedback from your audience. A wrinkled forehead or a shake of the head can suggest that the last point you made was not clear or that your audience is not "buying it." Your listeners may yawn, shift their weight in their seats, lift their feet, or play with the rungs of their chairs—all indications that you, the speaker, have lost them. They may nod in agreement and smile when you state something, showing that you have held their interest. The audience's responses will dictate the course of the speech, perhaps requiring you to rephrase a point or clarify information.

Your goal as a good speaker is to relay information in such a way that you gain and help keep the audience's attention. This can be done by keeping the specific purpose of your speech in mind, which will be covered in this unit. Your goal as an audience member is to be attentive and listen to the speaker's message so that you arrive at the result the speaker expects at the end of their speech. This result is formulated by the speaker in what is called a specific purpose statement and can help the speaker organize their speech in a fashion that will be understood by the audience.

Who Will Understand My Speech?

The result of completing step 1—picking a topic and narrowing it—and step 2—focusing by completing an audience analysis and a working plan—will allow you to create a clear statement that guides the rest of your speech-making process. If you can't state your speech topic clearly in one sentence, you won't be able to guide your audience to a specific end result effectively. This sentence is known as a specific purpose statement, step 3, and will be the guiding point for the rest of the speech-preparation steps.

A **specific purpose statement** is a single sentence that states the response you hope to elicit from the audience. In one simple sentence, you will state the intent and desired goal of your entire speech. A specific purpose statement reflects the speaker's interests, knowledge, and purpose, while taking into account the audience's interests, knowledge, and purpose. This statement comes from the focusing process and should follow three guidelines: A specific purpose statement:

1. must be written as a simple *complete sentence.*
2. must be worded *clearly* and *concisely.*
3. must state the expected *audience response.*

The first guideline, *must be written as a simple complete sentence,* means you must include one, and only one, subject in your statement. "The audience will be able to make a banana split" is a simple sentence with one subject and one verb. "The audience will be able to make a banana split and I will show them the best way to eat it" is a compound sentence with two subjects and two verbs and, therefore, doesn't meet the requirements of a specific purpose statement. You must be specific about the *ultimate* goal of your speech. That goal should be worded as one outcome, the outcome you want your audience to understand.

The second guideline, *must be worded clearly and concisely,* means your specific purpose should be easily read and understood. You should make your statement as short as possible and use words that say *exactly how you want the audience to react.* "The audience will know about the Federal Reserve System" is not worded clearly and concisely. It is written in the proper form, but it does not state precisely what the speaker wants his audience to know. What, specifically, about the Federal Reserve System does he want his audience to know? Should the audience know how or why it was formed, its purpose, what effect it has on our economy, or why it should be changed or abolished? A clear, specific purpose statement for an informative speech on this topic might be, "The audience will understand why the Federal Reserve System was founded." A specific purpose for a persuasive speech might be, "The audience will be convinced that the Federal Reserve System should be abolished."

The third guideline, *must state the expected audience response,* means your specific purpose statement should address what you want your audience to understand or do at the completion of your speech. "I will tell my audience to donate blood to the Red Cross" is not a proper specific purpose statement for a persuasive speech because it does not include a response from the audience. It states what the speaker will do, but it does not state what the audience will do. "The audience will donate blood during the next bloodmobile drive," states exactly what the speaker wants the audience to do. This may seem nitpicky, but there is an important reason for doing this.

When you state you are going to inform, tell, motivate, persuade, or convince your audience, you are referring to what you, as the speaker, will be doing in your speech. However, it doesn't require you to consider your audience. Writing a specific purpose statement forces you to consider all the information you gained from step 2, focusing, and states how you can help your audience achieve the goal you have established and ultimately understand your speech.

Examples

Remember that the subject of a specific purpose statement will be your audience; the audience will learn the knowledge or perform the action you wish at the conclusion of your speech. Consider the following examples:

- The audience will know how to change a flat tire.
- The audience will know how to register to vote.
- At the conclusion of my speech the audience will sign a petition against raising gasoline taxes.
- The audience will believe that the appeal process for convicted murderers should be shortened.
- The audience will be amused by my story about canoeing.

Specific purpose statements follow the same guidelines whether they are for speeches to inform, persuade, or entertain. However, because of the intent of the speaker, they may be worded differently (primarily the verb you choose will be different). When you are giving a speech in which the general purpose is to inform, the specific purpose statement can begin with any of the following: "The audience will know . . ." "The audience will understand . . ." "The audience will have a clear knowledge of . . ." In a speech to persuade, the specific purpose statement should begin with, "The audience will sign . . ." "The audience will donate . . ." and so forth.

It is important to note that you probably will not state your specific purpose statement during your speech. It is a tool to help you in creating your speech.

Strengthen Your Skills

Writing Specific Purpose Statements

Purpose: The purpose of this exercise is to give you practice in preparing different types of specific purpose statements.

Procedure:
Below you will find examples of specific purpose statements for focused speeches. Your task is to create another specific purpose for that same speech. Make sure it reflects the type of speech stated through the use of language:

Example:
Type of Speech: three- to five-minute informative speech

General Topic: Halloween
a.   The audience will know how to carve a jack-o-lantern.
b.   The audience will be able to make popcorn balls as treats for Halloween visitors.

Exercises:
1.   Type of Speech: 5- to 7-minute informative speech
     General Topic: Snow
     a.   The audience will know how to make a snowball.
     b.   (you fill this in)

2.   Type of Speech: 5- to 7-minute informative speech
     General Topic: Zoos
     a.   The audience will be aware of how the St. Louis Zoo is funded.
     b.   (you fill this in)

3.   Type of Speech: 7- to 10-minute persuasive speech
     General Topic: Cars
     a.   The audience will purchase an economy car rather than an SUV.
     b.   (you fill this in)

4.   Type of Speech: 7- to 10-minute persuasive speech
     General Topic: Cleaning
     a.   The audience will use environmentally friendly cleaners.
     b.   (you fill this in)

5.   Type of Speech: three- to five-minute special occasion speech
     General Topic: Introduction
     a.   The audience will be introduced to the school mascot.
     b.   (you fill this in)

(Continued)

6. Type of Speech: three- to five-minute special occasion speech
    General Topic: Vacations
    a. The audience will be amused by the mishaps that occurred on
        my trip to Washington, DC.
    b. (you fill this in)

You have now learned how to create a specific purpose statement and have completed step 3 of the nine-step speech process. Your specific purpose statement is a tool to help you know precisely what your speech goal is; reaching that goal is discussed in the next unit. But before we begin the next unit it is wise to consider that you may be starting to feel anxious about delivering your speech. Thinking about achieving that audience response and being at the podium may have you starting to experience some symptoms of anxiety and nervousness.

Who Is Experiencing Speech Anxiety?

For many, the nervous anticipation that they experience when they think about speaking to an audience is the worst part of preparing for a speech. Many beginning public speakers, as well as veteran speakers, encounter this rush of nerves. All that is physically required to speak effectively is the skill to connect our thoughts to our mouth—a skill that you already possess. The task you have as a speaker is to find the courage within yourself to use this skill to speak in front of an audience. Research has shown that in the United States alone, speaking in public is one of our greatest fears, preceded only by death and flying, for some! Why are we afraid? We often ask our students this question and are surprised by some of their answers. Some students fear that they will lose their voice; some are afraid they will trip on their way to the podium; some fear the audience will laugh at them, or think they are stupid. The primary concern that seems to emerge, however, is that the audience will reject their ideas.

Audience members are free to accept or reject whatever is presented to them at any given time. This thought might cause you, as a beginning speaker, to get nervous. After all, no one likes the idea of rejection for any reason. We become nervous and fear that others may not agree with us, or be inclined to ignore our viewpoint. This nervous fear is often referred to as **speech anxiety.** Speech anxiety creates psychological and physical symptoms such as dry mouth, shaking hands, or butterflies in your stomach. Some people get an extreme case of speech anxiety that can cause such intense reactions as sweating, shivering, or red splotches on the skin. It is important for you to know that, in your authors' combined teaching history spanning over 60 years, no one has fainted at the podium yet! Public speaking can, however, cause you significant anxiety. The key to controlling this anxiety is understanding what makes you anxious.

What most people really fear, as they take the podium the first few times, is they might appear foolish. Remember being called on to read out loud, one of the oldest horrors of childhood? You suffered the pangs of this fear in grade school when you were called on to read or recite an answer. Will I know how to pronounce all of the words? Will I have the right answer? Does my teacher like me? Will my friends tease me about it at recess? Despite whether you did your homework or not, you still were not certain you would get it right, and any public exposure made you sweat.

The same is true today, only you are older. Your exposure to the world has taught you that you can be disappointed, you are sensitive, and some people may attempt to hurt you. Now, take a look around the room at your assembled speech class. All of the other students in the room will be required to get up and make speeches—the instructor has this expectation. Are they likely to tease you? Is it feasible that they would wish to hurt you? If they are getting up at the podium, too, wouldn't it be possible that they will treat you as they would wish to be treated? Then, what is the real problem?

The problem is that we are human. We, as human beings, often tend to view the negative aspect of any situation first. The ability to overcome your fears and conquer speech anxiety rests with the ability to overcome the negative and focus on the positive. It is helpful to remember that your audience members are people, too. These people have a responsibility to be audience members and listen to what you have to say. They really do want to hear what you have to say and they want you to succeed. Nevertheless, those thoughts of failure may be floating around in your head, while the physical symptoms of speech anxiety begin to manifest. Even if you are able to conquer your thoughts, how can you control your body? What is actually happening inside your body when fear or nervousness strikes?

Symptoms of Speech Anxiety

You need to understand the physical reaction of your body when you are nervous if you want to be able to conquer your speech anxiety. What happens during an attack of nerves? Scientists have determined that **adrenaline,** a hormone produced by the body under stress, flows through your body. This powerful force surges through your body and must find an outlet. This is the same energy that can give you the added boost to run the 440 in 45 seconds. It is "the edge" coaches speak of in athletic competitions—the same energy that allows a runner to surge ahead from last place and win the race. This energy will not just go away; it must be used by the body. Unfortunately, our bodies choose to use adrenaline in several unattractive ways: we sweat, we shake, we turn red, or we have dry mouth. All of these are examples of physical reactions to the source of energy our body recognizes as adrenaline. Even professional actors and speakers suffer from this strange condition, often referring to it as **stage fright.** They describe in great detail how they had to overcome the opening-night jitters but then went on to rave reviews. After all, everyone knows the show must go on!

Strengthen Your Skills

Glossophobia is the technical term for speech anxiety or the fear of public speaking. While everyone may have some anxiety related to speaking to an audience, the following diagnostic tool will help you rate the level of your anxiety and suggest how much effort you may have to exert to manage it. Please try to be objective and honest in your answer to the following symptoms.

Rate the frequency you experience the following symptoms using the scale provided.

Always   Frequently   Sometimes   Rarely   Never

1. Immediate feeling of nervousness when first asked to deliver a speech.

2. Desiring to avoid giving the speech even if it means failing a class.

3. Immediately assuming things will go badly during the speech.

4. Thinking about being embarrassed or unprepared for your speech.

5. Feelings of self-doubt at the thought of delivering a speech.

6. Repeatedly asking yourself if you can actually get up and present a speech.

(Continued)

7. When delivering a speech how often do you experience a dry mouth?

8. When delivering a speech how often do you experience blushing or red splotches?

9.   When delivering a speech how often do you experience "butterflies in your stomach?

10. When delivering a speech how often do you experience actual nausea?

11. When delivering a speech how often do you experience cold hands or feet?

12. When delivering a speech how often do you experience a quivering vocal tone?

13. When delivering a speech how often do you experience stuttering or stammering?

14. When delivering a speech how often do you experience a rapid/racing heart beat?

15. When delivering a speech how often do you experience dizziness or feeling faint?

16. When delivering a speech how often do you experience shaky hands?

17. When delivering a speech how often do you forget what you were going to say?

18. When delivering a speech how often do you experience shaky knees?

19. When delivering a speech how often do you experience excessive perspiration?

20. When delivering a speech how often do you experience other symptoms that you label as nervousness not specifically included in this assessment?

Scoring:
> Always = 4 points
> Frequently = 3 points
> Sometimes = 2 points
> Rarely = 1 point
> Never = 0 points

(Continued)

Low anxiety: If you scored 20 points or fewer, you have little anxiety about public speaking. Your "fears" are ones that are less than typical and can easily be managed by making sure you have completed the 9 essential steps to preparing and delivering an effective speech.

Average anxiety: If you scored 21–35 points you aren't alone. This is the range most people find themselves in, indicating some feelings of anxiety that can affect the delivery of your speech. In addition to using the nine-step speech process to prepare your speech, you may need to employ other methods to reduce your symptoms of anxiety.

High anxiety: Scoring over 35 points indicates severe anxiety (or at least your perception of your anxiety is severe) that needs to be addressed if you are going to deliver a successful speech. The first step is to check your perception. Retake the assessment and objectively revisit those you rated as "Always." Most of you will find that always isn't really true. Picture yourself presenting your speech to an audience of friends and family who want you to succeed. In that circumstance would you still rate that item as "Always"? Next, make a list of the five items you rated highest and make a plan that includes specific actions you can take to decrease these characteristics. For example if you often forget what you were going to say, having easy to use notes will help tremendously. Then, follow through with your plan. Remember almost everyone experiences some speech anxiety and that's OK because it means you care about the outcome. Remember, with good preparation and a positive attitude you can deliver your speech successfully to your audience.

Who Can Overcome Speech Anxiety?

Do you know people who always seem confident and poised in any speaking situation? They are the ones who enter a room and seem immediately at ease, able to size up the situation and began speaking more confidently. Most of these people did not always behave in this manner. Often they began their speaking careers on as shaky a foundation as yours. They may have felt awkward, fearful, or unprepared, too. What separates them from you is that they have learned to overcome their speech anxiety.

There are several suggestions we can make that experienced speakers have used successfully to overcome their speech anxiety. The following five tips can help even the most inexperienced speakers feel more confident in any speaking situation.

1. ***Control your fears.***   Almost everyone fears the unknown. This is true as you walk to the podium. You fear not knowing how your speech will turn out. This is a perfectly natural reaction in this situation. You need to understand that although you cannot eliminate all of your anxiety, you can control the symptoms it creates.

2. ***Think positively.***   The mind is very powerful. We often cause situations to happen simply by believing they will happen. Deciding you can and will deliver an effective speech will take you a long way toward achieving your goal. Think positively and believe that you can get the job done.

3. ***Be prepared.***   Always pick a topic you are interested in and enthusiastic about. This eliminates doubts you might have if you were to speak about a topic with which you are unfamiliar. Do a complete job of audience analysis before each and every speech. By knowing your audience members' beliefs, opinions, and interests, you can prepare a speech that will keep their attention. You will also be better prepared to anticipate their possible reaction and make adjustments in your presentation if necessary. Prior to giving your speech, create the speech environment as much as you can and then practice for your performance. As you practice, imagine yourself walking confidently to the podium and looking at your audience. Enlist a few friends or family members to listen as you practice. Practice your speech aloud at least three times before your actual presentation. Then practice it again!

4. ***Focus on the audience.***   Concentrate on your audience to decrease your anxiety. Don't be afraid of making eye contact. Develop rapport and speak directly to them. Don't be afraid of making verbal mistakes. Everyone occasionally mispronounces a word, fails to define a term, or says "um" or "uh" instead of a word. Don't hesitate to be human. It is not necessary to call attention to your nervousness by apologizing; just continue with your speech. Studies show that audiences are much less aware of your mistakes than you think. Concentrating on your fear of making one will only increase the chance that you will actually make a mistake.

5. ***Learn from experience.***   You aren't the first person to experience speech anxiety. Everyone has had to deal with it at some time or another. Your instructor may not look nervous in front of the class, but that's because he or she has learned how to control

the fear. One of us always looked for the trash can before giving a lecture, because she knew she would be sick from nerves when she began to speak! Listen to what your instructors tell you and follow their suggestions. Concentrate on making your introduction flawless—fear is most intense at this time and will dissipate after you get started.

In addition to the five tips given above, it helps if you do not read or memorize your speech. While beginning speakers think this will decrease anxiety, it doesn't. If memory fails (and it usually does), anxiety will increase. Reading your speech leads to a boring speech. Imagine 50 first-graders reciting the pledge of allegiance from memory! Don't forget to make eye contact with your audience. This will allow you to pick up on their feedback. It will also give you encouragement from the nods, smiles, and other signs that your audience will be providing. Use visual aids to add interest and help you present your information. Explaining a chart or picture helps take your mind off your anxiety and gives you another physical outlet for adrenaline.

Once you have made it through your first speech, you will be more relaxed. You will know you can do it, and your future speeches will be much easier! Speech anxiety is real and expected. It means you care about the outcome of your efforts, and that, in itself, is positive. Despite what you may now believe about your future speaking engagements, you can and will make it through this public speaking class. Think positively, prepare, and practice so you can help yourself overcome your fears. We have a method that we often introduce to our students that seems to help. Let us introduce you to CEM! We have found this method to be invaluable in helping beginning speakers deal with speech anxiety.

The CEM Method

CEM is an acronym that stands for control, eliminate, and mask. Our method uses these three elements to help you *control* your anxiety, *eliminate* your symptoms, and *mask* your nervous behaviors. First you must identify what is actually causing your anxiety. For example, if adrenaline is causing knocking knees or shaking hands, then you could *control* them by channeling this energy into facial expressions, gestures, or dynamic vocal inflections. If your anxiety is caused by feeling unprepared, then you can *eliminate* that fear by researching, organizing, and practicing your speech until you feel comfortable with what you are saying. If your fears simply refuse to go away, you have to *mask* or hide them. One of your authors breaks out in red splotches when she gives a speech. Try as she might, she has been unable to get rid of them. They don't always appear, but when they do, her neck and chest are covered with them. Controlling and eliminating are not options. Therefore, she *masks* them by wearing a high-neck blouse or turtleneck when she's in a speaking situation that produces them! Now it's your turn to get to know CEM. Use it as a tool to help you overcome your speaking fears.

Strengthen Your Skills

Meet CEM

Purpose: Applying the CEM technique can help you be more at ease. Anxiety is a normal reaction to situations in which we don't know what the outcome will be, like giving a speech.

Procedure:
1. Create a list of five nervous symptoms you experience when faced with delivering a speech to a group of people.

2. Investigate each one and decide which ones will need control, elimination, or masking. You may find that you don't have to use all three. You may discover that you can eliminate many by practice and using a positive approach (believing you will do well).

3. Use suggestions from this chapter, talk to others to find out what they do about anxiety, or remember how you overcame it in the past in other situations. The symptoms of nervousness remain the same whenever we are afraid, so if you have been able to overcome anxiety in other situations, such as taking tests or when meeting a new group of people, using those techniques can work when you give a speech.

4. For each of your five symptoms, do the following:
State what part of CEM you believe will cover the problem.
Explain what you will do (be specific) for each symptom listed.

In the role of speaker, we need to anticipate and plan. If we don't, we often find ourselves unprepared for the situation at hand. Planning your speech decreases the likelihood that you will fail. Butterflies in the stomach, shaking hands, and a general feeling of anxiety are common ailments that novice speakers often experience. They need not spoil your speech. We've introduced you to CEM now it's your turn to put it in action.

Conclusion

While we may think of ourselves primarily in the role of speaker in a public speaking situation, we cannot discount the importance of the audience. We must make an effort to find out as much about our audience as we can through audience analysis. We can then create a working plan that will help us incorporate this new found information into the further development of our speech. It is important to consider how difficult it is for an audience to pay attention and listen. Developing our speech with the audience in mind can help them to be more attentive listeners. As a speaker you must be aware of things that distract others from listening. As an audience member, you must take the steps necessary to eliminate these distractions. Otherwise you will engage in poor listening habits and will miss the speaker's message. There are ways that we can keep ourselves from tuning out and improve our listening skills. By using these skills, we can become a good audience member and help the person speaking become a better speaker.

Giving an effective speech requires much more than just telling the audience something and having them listen. It demands that the speaker form a bond with the audience—that's what specific purpose statements can help you do. These statements will be valuable in helping you in the remaining steps of the speech process. As we continue preparing our speeches, we must consider the possibility of nervous anxiety. One way to control speech anxiety is by using the CEM method. Keeping our fears under control can help us feel confident while completing the remaining steps in the speech making process.

■ DISCUSSION QUESTIONS

1. As a member of the audience, what advice would you give a speaker that would help you be a more attentive listener?
2. As the speaker, what can you do to decrease noise (in all forms) to make it easier for you to have your message attended to by the audience?
3. What does it mean to have a poor listening habit?
4. Name two types of internal noise.

5. What distracts you personally and which of the suggestions that we have made can help you to overcome this distraction?
6. How can a specific purpose statement help you as a speaker?
7. How can a specific purpose statement help the audience?
8. How does speech anxiety affect you personally?
9. Name three physical symptoms of speech anxiety and supply a possible remedy for each.

■ KEY WORDS

adrenaline
antilistening behaviors
assumptions
attending
audience analysis
CEM
demographic data
evaluating
focus
habits
hearing
intrapersonal communication
message overload
needs

occasion
physiological needs
preoccupied
psychological data
psychological needs
responding
retaining
sensory mode
speaking environment
specific purpose
specific purpose statement
speech anxiety
stage fright
working plan

CONSEQUENTLY

? Hence Thus

Wherefore ?

HOW?

ACCORDINGLY

? Therefore?

Wherein Ergo So

How?

. . . organize your speech . . .
. . . research your speech . . .
. . . create presentation aids . . .
. . . step 4 . . . step 5 . . . step 6 . . .

- How Do I Begin My Speech?
- How Do I Organize My Speech?
- How Do I Prepare an Outline?
- How Do I Organize My Outline?
- How Do I End My Speech?
- How Do I Find Facts for My Speech?
- How Do I Plan My Research?
- How Do I Choose the Best Sources?
- How Do I Cite My Sources?
- How Do I Make My Speech Better?

Now that we have a specific purpose statement and know exactly in what direction we are headed for our speech we can continue with step 4 of the nine-step process, figuring out how to organize the speech. Most people spend a great deal of time working on the body of their speech. They are concerned with getting their main points across; yet they spend little time on the beginning (introduction) and ending (conclusion) of the speech. Research shows that a speaker must gain the audience's attention in the first few seconds of a speech. It also shows that an audience listens best to the beginning and the end of a speech. Even though the body of your speech will use most of your speaking time, the introduction and conclusion are extremely important and must be carefully developed.

How Do I Begin My Speech?

The **introduction** of your speech must be planned to ensure that you start your speech in a positive, productive manner. It should fill approximately 15 to 20 percent of your overall time limit. In this short time an introduction needs to be clever, creative, clear, and concise. An effective introduction must fulfill the following four criteria:

1. It should *grab* the audience's attention.
2. It gives the audience a reason to listen, as they are thinking, "What's in it for me?" (*WIFM*).
3. It establishes the *credibility* of the speaker.
4. It should *preview* the main points that will follow in the speech body.

Getting the audience's attention is vitally important to accomplishing your speaking goal. If you don't grab their attention and get them to listen to you at the beginning of your speech, chances are you won't be able to catch them later in your speech either. Your introduction should get your audience to pay attention to you. It's your job as a speaker to get them listening. Find an interesting way to introduce them to your topic, by using a **grabber** to gain their attention.

The second requirement for an effective introduction is **WIFM** (What's in it for me?). The "me" refers to the audience. You must assume that your audience is questioning whether they will gain anything by listening to your speech. By answering this question you can ensure that your audience will listen to you. WIFM lets you tell the audience that there will be a reward if they pay attention. For example, listeners might learn an inexpensive way to entertain their children or a new idea for that perfect date. You can't just make up a reward and expect it to be effective. The reward must be one the audience will want, so this is another instance in the speech process where an audience analysis pays off. Audience analysis allows you to discover the needs, wants, and desires the audience has that your speech can help fulfill. Using this information in your speech introduction catches your audience's attention up front and ensures they continue to listen.

The third part of an effective speech introduction focuses on *you*. You must make sure the audience perceives you as believable, or credible. Establishing your **credibility** is one aspect of an introduction that may seem like a stumbling block. A speaker's credibility can be established based on his or her knowledge of the subject. However, the audience's perception of the speaker's trustworthiness, and how they judge the speaker's personal appearance, also influence whether or not the audience believes the speaker to be credible. Speakers who take the time to establish their credibility up front are much more effective. Your credibility will continue to be built throughout your speech. However, you can help establish a foundation for it by explaining your competence about your subject in your introduction. What's your experience with this topic? Where did you get your information? Be honest and careful when presenting your information—don't distort, lie, or leave out vital information. Is this a hobby you have been doing since you were a child? Tell the audience. Is this a disease that you or a family member suffers from? Tell the audience. Is this something you have had an interest in for years and have done extensive research about? Tell the audience. This will provide your audience with accurate, reliable information and establish your credibility in the first few seconds of your speech. Your goal is to show them why listening to you is important. You want your audience to be concerned, excited, happy, or angry about your topic. This motivates them to continue to listen.

Finally, the last step of the introduction should be a statement that lists the main points of your speech. You should orally **preview** what is coming next so that your audience can follow your speech more easily. Remember, your audience does not have your speech notes. They are relying on you to provide them with accurate information in an easy to understand format. A preview statement can help the audience stay focused on your speech and understand the sequence of the information you are providing. Don't go into detail, that will happen in the body of your speech. A preview statement will also help you to determine the order of your speech body.

Creating an effective introduction requires that you complete all four steps of the process. This may seem impossible in such a relatively short time, but it isn't. It is often your attention grabber that is the most difficult item to develop. The following is a list of possible grabbers you could use to begin your speech but be as creative as you like—just make sure to place your grabber first, and that your entire introduction fulfills the four requirements you have just learned.

1. Give an example or tell a story.

    a. "My mother was driving to work; I was at school." "I was 12 years old the day the Twin Towers were destroyed."

    b. "Teaching someone how to do something often helps you realize what you know. I've been studying algebra and I have always thought I wasn't good at it. My younger brother is taking a beginning course and is struggling with his homework. I helped him by explaining the basic theories. I discovered that I really do understand algebra, after all. Teaching my brother helped me feel more confident about my own skills in math!"

2. Ask your audience a question.

    a. "Have you ever wondered if your great-grandchildren will live on the moon?"

    b. "Which city is considered the most haunted city in America?"

3. Use a quote.

    a. "'Don't try it! I've tried them all myself and they don't work.' This is what my uncle always said when he first spoke to new recruits at Great Lakes Naval Training Base."

    b. "As Mark Twain said, 'I have never let my schooling interfere with my education.'"

4. Refer to a historical event or date.

    a. "September 11, 2001, is no longer just a fall day. It is a day we, as Americans, will never forget."

    b. "It was on this day in 1775 that the American Revolution began. A single shot fired at Concord Bridge became a shot heard round the world."

5. Tell a joke. (Make sure it is related to your topic.)

    a. For a speech on shearing sheep, you might start with, "Where do sheep get their hair cut? At baaaber shops."

    b. If you are giving a speech on the importance of enunciating your words and speaking clearly, you might start with, "As a high school graduate was running through the school grounds he yelled, 'I'm free, I'm free!' A child playing nearby responded, 'Big deal! I'm four!'"

6. State an unusual fact.

    a. "Your neighbor, your friend, a member of your family—one out of every two people in America is emotionally disturbed or mentally ill."

b. "By the year 2020, one out of four adults will have, or know someone with cancer."

7. Use a gimmick (a novelty opening).

   a. Do a sleight-of-hand trick that changes a dollar bill into thirty- five cents to begin a speech on inflation.

   b. Dress as Count Dracula for a speech on blood donation or vampires.

8. Refer to the purpose of your gathering. This works best when the audience is already emotionally aroused about the topic, such as a school board meeting or company sales meeting.

   a. "Five children have been injured while crossing the street in front of this grade school. We must have patrolled crosswalks. Our children's futures, maybe their lives, depend on it!"

   b. "February is the month for love. Valentine's Day is the most profitable day in the floral business. We can sell even more flowers if we promise that we are selling love."

Strengthen Your Skills

The Introduction

Purpose: The purpose of this exercise is to learn how to prepare a speech introduction that uses all four criteria we have learned.

Procedure:

1. Bring a short news article or magazine article to class (or the instructor may hand out articles).

2. Select one of the eight grabbers and prepare an introduction for your article. Make sure it fulfills all four requirements for an effective introduction.

3. The introduction should be 40 seconds to one minute in length and cannot start with, "My speech is about . . ."

4. Present the introduction orally in class.

Now that you have an idea about how you want to begin your speech, it is time to focus on the body of the speech. This is where the majority of your time as well as your information will be devoted. The key to developing a well-prepared speech is organization, and organizing your speech means arranging it in a way that is easy for your audience to follow. The best way to organize your speech is to create an outline for your ideas. This outline will become the map to help guide the rest of the nine step process.

How Do I Organize My Speech?

We've often heard students say, "I can prepare a speech, but I can't do the outline until last." Quite honestly, this is backwards! **Outlining** is the process used to achieve the goal of speech organization. Those who skip this process usually present a speech that rambles and is difficult to follow. Learning to prepare an outline can provide these advantages.

- The information in your speech becomes more familiar as you organize it, helping you to remember your speech material.
- You will be more relaxed, knowing you are organized and prepared.
- Your audience will be able to follow what you say because your speech moves logically from point to point, helping them listen.
- A proper organizational pattern creates a natural adjustment mechanism that lets your audience process information more easily.
- Your audience will remember what you say because organized information makes sense.

There are several types of outlines. **Working outlines** are used when you are working on your speech. They help you organize your ideas by putting your information in writing. They can help you determine what to include as support for the points of your speech. A working outline may be a series of phrases you have jotted down during the preparation process as you analyze your audience or do your research. These outlines can be created in any way you choose that is easy for you to follow. Your working outline will probably be seen only by you and does not need to follow any specific style.

A **speaking outline** is the outline you will take to the podium. Speaking outlines are also personal. Again, you can use any format that works best for you. Using an outline at the podium can help jog your memory and keep you from rambling while speaking. In addition, you can write notes to yourself about delivery, write transition words between points, or make notations about sources and citations.

A **formal outline** is the one you will most likely be required to present to your instructor when you actually deliver your speech. A formal outline must conform to certain rules. The main points of your speech are noted by Roman numerals (I, II, III). The subpoints of your speech are noted by capital letters (A, B, C). Further subpoints are noted by Arabic numbers (1, 2, 3), and any further division by lowercase letters (a, b, c). If you find it necessary to divide a point further, it probably means that your point is too broad and needs to be more clearly focused.

The most common mistake made by beginning speakers is trying to include too much information in the body of their speech. In our collective experience and research, the body of your speech should contain no less than three main points and no more than five main points. These main points will be represented by Roman numerals in your formal outline. Concentrate on the most important points that you need to convey to your audience, based on your audience analysis, and then develop each of them fully. This will result in a thorough and organized outline.

How Do I Prepare an Outline?

We suggest that all outlines should list your speech's specific purpose statement first. Then, when preparing a formal outline, you must label the three major parts of your presentation, the introduction, the body, and the conclusion. This assures that you have considered the purpose of each section of the speech. In addition, you should list your **bibliography** (sources) on your outline. A formal speech outline looks like the one below:

When selecting the main points of your speech, you must take into account the primary (most important) sections of your speech. They should be equal in importance and fill about the same amount of time in

---

Formal Speech Outline

Introduction
  I. *Grabber:* get the audience's attention.

  II. *WIFM:* gives the audience a reason to listen, "What's in it for me (the audience)?"

  III. *Credibility:* establish that the audience can trust you and believe you.

  IV. *Preview:* state the main points that will follow in your speech body

(Continued)

Body
  I.   Main point #1
       Subpoints
  II. Main point #2
       Subpoints
  III. Main point #3
       Subpoints
(continue until all points are listed, with no more than five)

Conclusion
  I.   Review: by repeating your preview statement
  II. Leaver: a statement that refers to your grabber and lets the
       audience know you are finished

Bibliography
  I.   Source #1
  II. Source #2
  III. Source #3
(continue listing all sources until completed)

your presentation. *Example:* You are giving a speech about purebred cats. The main points in the body of your speech might look like this:

  I. Siamese
  II. Persian
  III. Himalayan

Subpoints (capital letters—A, B, etc.) would then be added and would represent a division of your main points; as they further explain those points. These should also be of equal importance to each other and relate specifically to the heading under which they fall. In the same way, further subpoints (Arabic numerals—1, 2, etc.) fill the requirement of dividing the category under which they fall. The process of outlining involves breaking down broad ideas into smaller ones. Each time you divide an idea you must break it down into at least two parts. Simply stated, this means that every time you have a I, you must have at least a II; if you have an A, you must have a B; for every 1 there must be a 2.

Occasionally, you may find that some of your supporting material does not easily fall into two or more sections. When this occurs you simply identify the material under its heading. This is done with labels such as *example, story, quotation, definition, or visual aid*—followed by a colon, and the material itself. Here is an example:

A. Helping others
   Quotation: President Barack Obama on volunteering in one's community.

Each division or point on your outline should list only one idea. Don't put two or more ideas together. It's best to list your topic, general purpose, and your specific purpose statement on your outline. Let's look at an example of how the previously discussed guidelines for a formal speech outline might look.

Formal Speech Outline for "How to Change a Flat Tire"

Topic: How to Change a Flat Tire
General Purpose: Informative Speech
Specific Purpose: The audience will know how to change a flat tire.

Introduction
  I. *Grabber:* Tell my story about changing a tire in freezing weather without a jack.

  II. *WIFM:* Knowing how to change a tire can save you time and money in the future.

  III. *Credibility:* I have had to change a flat tire six times.

  IV. *Preview:* Having the right equipment and knowing the procedure for changing a flat tire can save you from freezing.

Body
  I. Equipment
     A. Tire Tool
     Visual Aid: show tool
     B. Jack
        1. Type A (bumper)
        2. Type B (scissors)
     C. Spare Tire

(Continued)

II.   Procedure
   A.   Secure Vehicle
      1.   Pull car off road
      2.   Make car immovable
         a.   Put in park
         b.   Block wheels
      Example: blocks or bricks
   B.   Remove Flat
      1.   Remove hubcap
      2.   Loosen lug nuts
      3.   Jack up car
      4.   Remove tire
   C.   Replace Tire
      1.   Put wheel on rim
      2.   Replace lug nuts
      3.   Release jack
      4.   Tighten lug nuts
      5.   Replace hubcap
   D.   Finish
      1.   Put equipment away
      2.   Remove wheel blocks

III.   Follow-up
   A.   Go to the nearest service station
      1.   Have lug nuts tightened
      2.   Check air pressure in spare
      3.   Have flat fixed
   B.   Replace spare with fixed tire

Conclusion
I.   Now you know the equipment and procedure for changing a tire.
II.   Follow these steps and you won't be left in freezing weather with a
      flat tire like I was!

Bibliography
Source 1
Source 2, etc.

Notice the form of the outline, where to indent, and when to capital-
ize. Outlines can be written using words and phrases or full sentences.
Most people find the word/phrase outline easier, but many beginning
speakers like the added security of a full-sentence outline.

An outline of a speech is much like a map. You want it to be clear. Your outline maps and directs the flow of your speech and includes all the information you will use to achieve your specific purpose. There are many organizational patterns that can help you outline and order your speech.

How Do I Organize My Outline?

There are many ways of organizing the main points of your outline. The most important thing to remember is to prepare your outline so that your speech will move from point to point in a logical manner—one that is easy for your audience to follow. Here are possible **organizational patterns** you can use for your speech.

Chronological organization organizes your material in a specific time frame. What occurred first, second, third? You move from the first occurrence to the most recent occurrence. If you were speaking on the development of our money system, chronological divisions might look like this:

I. English Money

II. Colonial Money

III. Modern Money

All the divisions are organized in time order, whether by minutes, months, or years.

Spatial organization uses divisions that are made according to geographical areas or space. If you were speaking about taking a trip from New York to California, spatial divisions might be:

I. Leave eastern seaboard

II. Drive to Midwest

III. Continue through mountains

IV. Arrive on West Coast

Remember, spatial divisions involve progressing from place to place or geographical location.

Process organization is used when you wish to follow a series of step-by-step actions. An outline showing the process for how to bake a cake could be handled in this way:

I. Read the recipe

II. Collect the ingredients and utensils

III. Mix the ingredients

IV. Bake the cake

V. Serving suggestions

Any topic that requires step-by-step action can be organized using a process division.

Priority organization separates items by importance, least to most important or vice-versa. You must decide how to prioritize your points. An outline on dental hygiene, organized by what you believe to be the most important element and finishing with the least important, could look like this:

I. Brushing

II. Flossing

III. Rinsing

Causal organization shows a relationship between the cause and effect of a topic. This type of pattern is often used for persuasive speeches to show what needs to be changed to bring about a particular result. An outline for a speech on the effects of viewing TV violence might look like this:

I. Children's television programs can contain a high percentage of violence.

II. Studies show that viewing violence affects children's behavior.

III. Violent crimes are increasing among children.

Problem solution organization discusses certain changes that need to occur and then offers a solution to achieve these changes.

I. Waste products are consuming our planet.

II. There are better methods for getting rid of waste.

III. These methods could help our environment.

These are just a few of the ways you can divide and organize your topic. You might want to consider the pros and cons of each, choosing the one that works best and is the most relevant to your topic. Just make sure that the pattern you choose helps the flow of your speech. The speech must move logically and smoothly from point to point.

How Do I End My Speech?

Now that you have thought about how to begin your speech and what you will say during it, you must create a **conclusion.** Since this is the last thing your audience will hear, you want to leave them with a clear statement so they will remember the main points of your speech. A conclusion should take about the same amount of time as your introduction. An effective conclusion must fulfill two criteria:

1. It should clearly remind the audience of your topic and main points.
2. It notifies the audience that you have finished your speech.

Just as your introduction informs your audience members what you are going to tell them, your conclusion tells them that you have said it. You should make a clear statement that reviews the main points of your speech. Conclude your speech in a way that will make clear to the members of your audience what you wanted them to learn, or do. You want them to remember specific points. Don't leave them guessing.

Let your audience know that you are finished speaking. Don't say, "That's about it, are there any questions?" Don't add any new information in your conclusion. Once you've started your conclusion and signaled a stop, tie it up (even if you left out some point when you were speaking). Your final statement can be prepared in the same way as your grabber. You can conclude with any of the following, so choose a creative ending.

1. Give an example.
2. Ask a question.
3. Use a quote.
4. Refer to a date.
5. Tell a joke.
6. State a fact.
7. Use a gimmick.
8. Refer back to the purpose of your gathering.

The last thing you must include in your outline is your list of sources. This should be done in standard bibliography format. The number of sources you need for a particular speech will vary.

With a well-organized outline, the body of your speech can serve as the map that guides your research and can further be used to help you

Strengthen Your Skills

The Conclusion

Purpose: The purpose of this exercise is to learn how to prepare a speech conclusion.

Procedure:

1. Bring a short news article to class (or the instructor may hand out articles to read).

2. Referring to the different ways to end a speech in this unit, prepare a conclusion for the article. Make sure it fulfills the two criteria.

3. The conclusion should be 40 seconds to one minute in length.

4. Present the conclusion in class.

prepare your speech notes for your final presentation. Here is a summary of what to do to write an outline:

1. Decide how you might want to begin your speech.
2. Decide on your main points.
3. Divide the main points, where necessary, into further subcategories.
4. Decide on an organizational pattern.
5. Add your conclusion, and sources.

How Do I Find Facts for My Speech?

Having a properly prepared outline does not mean you have finalized your speech. How will you discuss your main points? How will you find information that you can use to support your ideas? Your outline can be used as a "map" that will help guide you in finding facts for your speech. You can gather the information you need through the process of research, which is step 5 of the nine-step process.

Research is the process of gathering credible information for your speech. This research supports your ideas, and gives the audience a reason to believe what you say. This part of the speech process is vitally important if you are going to be an effective speaker. It's also something that most people either spend too little or too much time doing. This unit will help you learn the "Goldilocks approach," or "the just right" approach, to research and its many facets.

Contrary to many students' opinions, time spent learning and verifying facts, clarifying ideas, and finding examples during the research process will save you time in speech preparation. Though you may believe you're well informed about your topic, you will find that you still need to research. You may need to do an experiment, gather data, read about a peace treaty, verify the wording of a law, or check an ingredient in Mom's prize-winning recipe. You may need a chart, story, or recording to help clarify, explain, or add interest to your speech. Whatever your speech is about, adding information to what you already know will help you decide what else you need to include. You may discover that some material is not as important as you thought, or discover you neglected to include some major or interesting point.

Perhaps the most important answer to the question, "Why do I need to research something I already know about?" is to verify that what you believe is actually factual. While many people assume their opinions are the same as facts, they aren't. Opinions can, and should be based on factual information. You will need to research the information you are going to deliver in your speech to make sure you are being truthful. In addition, facts can and do change. New discoveries are made, archeological evidence is found, or other evidence previously unknown is presented, and what was known as a fact is now fiction. For example, your authors are willing to bet that a significant number of you were taught that Pluto was a planet! Not anymore! Facts can change, and it is the research process that provides the data you need to assure yourself and your audience that you are being truthful and that the information you are presenting is based on fact, not opinion.

How Do I Plan My Research?

We're busy people. We don't even want to pull over and wait for our fast-food order. Have you have stopped the microwave at the last 10 seconds because that was just too much longer to wait? If your answer is yes, you probably think you don't have the time to spend planning research when you can just boot up and start Googling.

It's time to confess. How many times have you rushed into something without thinking it through and regretted it? How many times have you had to make an additional trip to complete a chore you forgot about when you were out earlier in the day? How many times have you had to do something over because you didn't follow directions the first time? How much time have you wasted because you failed to plan before doing something? Your authors think that collectively we have probably wasted several years of our lives. Taking time to prepare a research plan now will save you time later! In a **research plan,** you consider what information you need, why you need it, and where you are likely to find it. An effective research plan will address three general areas:

1. *The Topic:*   What information you need.
2. *The Audience Analysis:*   Why you need it.
3. *The Data:*   Where you can find it.

While your authors suggest you take time (probably only a few minutes) to write out your research plan, this step can be done mentally. The format you use is your choice since no one will see it except you (unless your instructor wants a copy). For each area of your plan, you will need to ask yourself several questions. The answers to these questions will direct your research.

The Topic

By this time in the process you should have created a specific purpose statement that considers you, the audience, and the occasion, and have created an outline that lists the main ideas you want to use in your speech. If you haven't done so, you aren't ready to do research. When you are ready, ask yourself the following questions:

1. What is the overall or general topic of my speech?
2. What is the specific topic of my speech?
3. What are other related topics?
4. What else could these topics be called?

The purpose of considering these questions is to give you an idea of the kind of sources you might need to find. Knowing what else a topic can be called will help you decide whether you are going online, heading to a museum, or planning an interview. Knowing your

specific topic will help you fine-tune exactly what you need to search for once your general topic is located. Knowing other related topics can help expand a search that isn't providing what you need. Knowing other names for a topic will help you find additional information more easily by giving you multiple keywords to use for your search. We've known students who insist (and we believe them) that they have spent hours trying to find two or three sources to support a five- to seven-minute speech, yet can't find anything about their topic. They often think they have to change their topic and start all over again! They're frustrated and angry that they've wasted so much time. As their teachers, we ask if they took the time to prepare a research plan. The answer is usually no, because if they had, they would have realized that their topic could be called many things. We have frequently found that when we type in a different word for their topic in our favorite search engine, we are rewarded with a multitude of Web sites that offer valuable and credible information.

The Audience

Previously we emphasized the importance of an audience analysis. If you did one for your topic, then answering the questions related to this step should be easy. If you can't answer these questions, go back and look at your audience analysis again. If you don't have enough information to answer these questions, you must seek additional information about your audience before you can continue with your research. You should be able to answer these questions to guide your research plan at this step:

- What knowledge does my audience already have about my topic?
- What does my audience need to know that I can provide?
- How can I keep my audience interested?

Since these are similar questions to those you asked in your audience analysis, you should find you already have enough information for this part of the research plan. Knowing how much your audience knows about your topic will help you focus your search for specific materials. If your topic is one your audience already knows something about, you must find new information that is unfamiliar to them.

Knowing what your audience's needs are is an essential ingredient for any effective speech. Not only is this the way you get their attention initially (WIFM), but it is how you maintain it throughout your speech. Where can you find the information that will fulfill their needs? What kind of support is required to convince your audience that your speech will provide them with a reward? This is where you might use that list of related topics you generated in the first step of your research plan. If your topic is saving money, what additional information might help you get your audience to realize the need to save—maybe the cost of housing or food in the future?

Finally, consider finding any additional information that can keep your audience interested in your topic. Would a clever quote, poem, or example help? Where are you likely to find sources for these elements? Would a pie chart help explain those numbers you need to include? Do you need an audio clip to help your audience understand what you are explaining? Would a list of Web sites be an appropriate handout, or do you need clear directions on how to make a recipe? Did PBS or NPR broadcast a show about your topic? Did you record it? Can it be found on their Web site? Considering what you need to enhance your speech, and doing the research it takes to find the information, makes it much more likely that you can keep your audience interested.

A research plan will help you discover the specific information you need to establish to support the main points of your topic. You will not waste time reading page after page of information that repeats what you already know.

The Data

After you have answered the questions about the topic and the audience, you should have a clear idea of the *specific* information you need to enhance your topic. In fact, if you have done a *thorough* analysis of the topic and the audience, you may not need to complete this section of your research plan at all. This part of the plan lists possible sources you need to check to support your speech and establish credibility.

Even if you have mentally thought through the previous two steps, it's a good idea to write down the answers to the following questions:

- What sources will provide the information I need?
- Where will I find them?
- How much time should I allow to find this information?

Since you have most likely chosen a topic you are interested in and know something about, chances are you already know some specific sources to check. Write them down. Can this be a "one-stop" shopping trip? Can you get the information you need online or is a trip to the local library necessary? Is an interview of a friend appropriate? Plan it out. Make sure you provide yourself adequate time to complete the actual research once you know what it is you wish to find. This is the "tricky" step in finding the "just right" plan. You want to plan enough time to find your credible sources but not spend more time than necessary.

We started this unit by discussing our busy lives, so it seems obvious that your research plan should include a step that considers how much time will be needed to complete your research. Also consider how much time you will need to read, analyze, organize, and prepare the information you gather into an effective speech. Try to make a good estimate of how much time needs to be allotted for each aspect of the research. If you have adequately focused your topic, it won't take you long to prepare a research plan. Thirty minutes or less will find you with a plan in hand that will save you an enormous amount of time during your research-gathering sessions.

Creating a realistic plan and follow through with that plan. A realistic plan is one that considers not only how much time it will take to research, but also how you can fit that time into your schedule. A realistic plan doesn't spend more time on research than necessary. Once you have your plan in hand, you will find that there are many types of support you can use for your speech. The following is a list of the types of support you might look for while doing research for your speech:

- Examples, facts, or statistics
- Illustrations, comparisons, or descriptions
- Graphs, charts, or tables
- Opinions, testimony, or quotations

The next sections offer ways to get the support items listed above.

The Internet

We are going to assume that the majority of you use the **Internet** on a daily basis. We suspect that you use it to check your email, your Facebook page, chat with friends, or see what's new on your favorite site. If so, you've already used it for researching some of the types of support listed above.

Your authors, having completed our degrees when a web was something a spider made, have nonetheless whole heartedly embraced the opportunities the World Wide Web provides. We can stay at home and teach our classes in our pajamas, or communicate with our friends, coworkers, and students online. We encourage you to use this valuable source as well. However, before you boot up and start Googling, remember that finding good sources takes more than a search engine. The Internet is only one of several ways to find support for your speech, but we will address it first.

Why travel to a library when the computer in my home office can provide everything I need? To this we say, indeed! But just because information is available, it doesn't mean all of that information is credible or reliable. The Internet is not really tangible, it's not a place; it's an idea. It consists of a very large number of people, all over the globe connected to phone lines, cell towers, cable, and satellites through their computers. They have generated vast amounts of data and information that is just waiting for you, 24 hours a day, 365 days a year. Yet, much of what is out there is personal opinion and not factual information.

Search engines and directories provide easy ways of finding information about your topic. These free services search the Internet for you to find sites that match the topic/keywords you have entered. You can choose and access the ones you want. It's easy and very user-friendly. Yet, don't assume that the sites listed first are the best.

You may already know an **Internet address** also known as a URL (uniform resource locator), find one in a magazine, or see one on TV. Carefully copy the *entire* address *exactly* as it appears. Your web browser can take you to the site only if you give it the right address. You'll find dictionaries, newspapers, encyclopedias, magazines, and much more. You can surf to the White House, tour the Smithsonian, or search libraries all over the world. While the Internet is a potential source for vast amounts of information, you shouldn't believe everything you read there. As a researcher it is your responsibility to verify the credibility of your sources. We'll talk about how to do that later in this unit.

Personal Experiences

You may not qualify as the world's leading authority on welfare reform, or the mating habits of tigers, but you have probably accumulated a great deal of knowledge during your lifetime. **Personal experience** is the ideal starting point for gaining support for your speech. If you've chosen a topic you are interested in, that probably means you have some knowledge about it. Indeed, you may be the primary source for some speeches you will give. You could talk about dealing with stress while going to school, working, and taking care of a family. You could explain how to change the oil in a car or how to install new software on a computer if you have already done these things. If you've dealt with a topic and have experience with it, your personal knowledge is certainly a valid source for your speech. Although it's a good starting point, your experience probably isn't complete enough to serve as your only source.

People you know and interact with every day can also be wonderful sources for your speech. Suppose you are talking about the Vietnam War. You are probably too young to personally remember that time in our nation's history. How can you understand and convey, the mood of our country during this time? You might know someone who was there, and his or her recollections could add valuable information to your speech. In fact, real human experiences are much more interesting than statistics or dry historical facts. Take advantage of the wealth of information available to you from people you see and talk to every day.

Interviews

Conducting an **interview** is a research method by which you question people who are knowledgeable in a field of study. This allows you to take advantage of expert opinions and knowledge. Interviews can be conducted in person, over the phone, by email, via Skype or a similar service, or through numerous social media sites. Interviews are an excellent source to use for information that might not be available from other sources.

If you are conducting a face-to-face interview, don't just stop by someone's office. Call, text, or email him or her and request an interview. Make an appointment. Explain who you are and why you want the interview. This initial contact also provides an opportunity for you to ask if you can record the interview. Do your homework; find out about your expert interviewee, and decide what information you need from him or her. Don't arrive at the interview and say, "Tell me what you know about gardening." Rather, ask questions that relate directly to your speech and the interviewee's knowledge. It is a good idea to write down any questions that you want to ask before you go to the interview. Sending them to your interviewee in advance is the best method to allow him or her time to prepare for your visit. That way, you will not waste time and will be well organized. Take notes on what is said even if you are recording the conversation (machines sometimes fail to work). Pay attention to the clock and try not to take up more time than was scheduled. Be sure to thank the person for the interview and give him or her credit as one of your sources in your speech and on your outline in your bibliography.

Surveys

Surveys are designed to gather information from people. A survey asks specific questions relating to a specific topic. Surveys may request factual data or ask for opinions. Developing a survey requires some work and attention to detail. Survey questions can be written in many different ways, depending on why you are asking them. You can ask questions that require only a "yes" or "no" answer or you can give the respondent a choice of multiple answers. In addition to questions that address your specific topic, you should ask questions pertaining to a respondent's demographic background (i.e., age, occupation, gender, etc.). Demographic information provides a helpful means of categorizing the answers you receive.

You will also have to select a sample group (people whom you will question) that are representative of the population you want to know about. Looking for opinions on voting? You can probably find a representative sample of voters at your church, civic organization, or even in your speech class. How many responses do you need? While the answer to this question depends on several factors, a good rule of thumb is to try to get as many responses as you can. For a speech, about 100 people is a good goal.

Pretest your questions with a few people to see if they understand your directions and questions. Make any changes necessary before you administer the survey to your targeted sample group. It's also a good idea to let your instructor check your survey before distributing it to your group.

Surveys take time to prepare, distribute, and tabulate. Nevertheless, they provide a good way to collect current information. If you can't take time to prepare and conduct a survey, check for surveys that have already been done. A survey can be very helpful if you need to know what people are thinking about a particular topic.

Media Sources

We live in what has been dubbed the Information Age. In addition to the Internet, we have access to information via other **media.** Television, radio, DVDs, and CDs are present in practically every home in

America. Workplaces often allow employees access to the media, and the commute to and from any destination can be accompanied by the car radio or listening to podcasts. In fact most Americans owe a great deal of what they know to cable and network news and other network and cable shows. Although, not all of what is broadcast is correct, information you obtain from these sources, if checked with another source, can provide useful support for your speech.

We have heard many interesting and creative approaches to speeches that involved music, actual recordings of news events, quotes, or vocal dramatizations. It is one thing to read about a certain type of music, but quite another to hear the actual music. Think about how powerful it would be to listen to an announcer describe an actual event as it takes place. In the past we would have needed to know in advance when such an event was taking place and make arrangements to record it. Today, TV and radio shows have searchable databases on their Web sites that can quickly provide you with these kinds of sources without you having to worry about recording anything (although setting up a recording is still a viable option).

Museums and Other Centers

If you live near a metropolitan area, the city is full of places to do research and have fun at the same time. Museums dedicated to art, history, and thousands of other topics are tucked away in cities all over the country. Even smaller towns have museums that can be used for research purposes. Science centers are often interactive and provide data on all sorts of topics. Zoos and aquariums are filled with information about animals and aquatic life. All these places can provide you with useful material for your speeches. Find out the names and addresses of the sources that are relevant to your speech and visit or locate their Web sites. Take a virtual tour to gain useful data for your speech.

Organizations and Businesses

There are local, regional, national, and international organizations and businesses dedicated to the pursuit and distribution of information on just about any topic. These groups usually publish newsletters, pamphlets, or brochures about their area of interest and expertise. Frequently they can provide up-to-date information that may be difficult to find elsewhere. They have their own Web sites, loaded with valuable data. If you don't know the names of organizations that would be useful in your search, go to the library or do a search online and find the *Encyclopedia of Associations* or the *Directory of Nonprofit Organizations*. These directories will list addresses, Web sites, email contact information, and phone numbers. A word of caution is necessary about information you may obtain from these companies or organizations. These groups have a personal stake in their subject; therefore, the information you receive may be biased and should not be used as your only source. Statistics and facts should be verified with other sources to help you establish credibility with your audience.

The Library

Remember that place with all the books? Don't forget the advantages that a library can provide. The reason a library exists is to provide multiple sources of information at one convenient location. Libraries are very user-friendly, and librarians are knowledgeable people who are there to assist you. If you don't know where to start or are having difficulties, ask the librarian. Just don't expect him or her to do your research for you; that's your job.

How Do I Choose the Best Sources?

While your research plan should have helped you decide what types of support you need for your speech, and we have examined the various sources available to find that support, you still need to consider what you will include in your speech. What information will be the most effective in helping to establish your credibility? What will interest your audience and substantiate what you say? In comparing information that we have found in numerous articles, textbooks, and other research, we believe that there are five criteria you should consider when deciding what research to use in a speech.

1. *Age.*   Recent examples, events, quotes, or occurrences are best. Sources should be no more than two years old with the exception of historical references.

2. *Relevancy.*   Information should correspond directly to your topic and audience to allow them to make the connection between what you say and their own lives.

3. *Significance.* Don't use something just because it was the first support you found. The material should be relevant (see #2) and should support the points of your speech.

4. *Variety.* Use many different kinds of support to provide more diverse information and keep the interest of your audience.

5. *Suitability.* Consider your audience, the occasion, and any directions you have been given by your instructor or the person who requested that you speak. This way you can avoid any negative reactions to your speech.

We first discussed credibility as a necessary part of an effective speech introduction. We stated that in the introduction you must inform the audience as to why they can trust and believe what you say. This is further accomplished by including citations in the body of the speech that add support, or credibility, to the information you have shared or to the persuasive arguments you have presented. Your credibility as a speaker is a significant factor in delivering an effective speech, and *your* credibility relies primarily on the credibility of your sources. While this has been true since the first person gave the first speech to an audience, it has become more complicated since the arrival of the Internet. Anyone can create a Web site and post whatever they choose on it, and their web content may or may not be fact. You'll need to verify whether the information is true. Is an expressed opinion supported by facts? How can you be sure the references, examples, and sources you have chosen are credible?

How Can I Be Sure My Sources Are Credible?

Doing a credibility check is as simple as A, B, C, D.
Consider the following information when determining if a source is credible:
Authority—Author's experience or knowledge that qualifies him or her as a valid expert.
Bias—Implied or stated political or ideological preferences.
Content/Currency—Depth of the material supplied, quality and age of information.
Design—Layout and user-friendliness of a site or other source.
This is the ABCD method of checking whether a source is credible.
Here is a checklist for evaluating information when using the ABCD method.

(Continued)

Authority	Yes	Can't Decide	No
Can you identify who is providing the information?			
Is a specific author cited for the works?			
Are the author's credentials/biography provided?			
Is the author known in his or her field of expertise?			
Is the author's area of expertise related to your topic?			
Do you recognize the author's name or works from other sources?			
Are the author's sources cited?			
• Is the publisher a reliable, well-known source?			
• If online, is the site a .gov, or .edu?			
Bias			
There are no preferences for political or ideological beliefs?			
Is the purpose of the information clearly stated?			
Can you identify the target audience for the material?			
Site is not a .com (commercial site designed to sell something)?			
Can you identify the goals or guidelines of the organization?			
Are the goals unbiased?			
Are diverse viewpoints represented?			
Opinions are supported with facts.			
Information does not come from a blog or other comment area?			
Content/Currency			
Does the source provide a well-rounded overview of the subject?			
Is a high level of detail provided?			
• Does the source provide verifiable facts?			
Opinions of the author or publisher are clearly labeled?			

(Continued)

• Data or references provided are credible?			
• No errors in grammar, spelling, or sentence construction?			
• Information less than 2 years old (except historical fact)?			
• Web site updated within the past 12 months?			
Design (primarily for Web sites)			
Is the Web site attractive?			
Is the Web site easy to navigate?			
• Recognizable logo or masthead?			
• Site is part of another reputable site (like a college)?			
Contact information for the webmaster present?			
• Contact Information for the content owner present?			
Has the site been favorably reviewed?			
Has the site won any awards?			

The more "yes" items you have checked in each category, the greater the chance the source you are evaluating is credible. If you have less than half the questions checked yes in each category, you may be running the risk of including unreliable or incorrect information in your speech if you choose to use the source.

When you choose sources, check their accuracy by using the ABCD checklist. Remember, the effectiveness of your speech depends on your credibility as a speaker. Your credibility depends on the credibility of your sources, and you alone are ultimately responsible for the accuracy of the facts in your speech.

How Do I Cite My Sources?

It is important to give credit where credit is due. Researchers spend many hours validating and publishing their ideas. It is important to pay tribute to their commitment. You will need to cite your sources in two ways for

Strengthen Your Skills

Scavenger Hunt

Purpose: To give you experience finding credible sources to support your speech points.

Procedure:

Use the Internet or the library to find a source that gives you the answers to these questions. Explain why you believe the source to be credible using the ABCD method.

1. When and where was the first performance of Bizet's *Carmen*?

2. What does *mellifluous* mean?

3. Who was Isak Dinesen?

4. Where is the Jutland Peninsula located?

5. Who was Felix Frankfurter?

6. What is the official name of what is commonly referred to as Obamacare?

7. In what month and year did the Phoenix Mars Mission locate ice on Mars?

8. How tall is the Eiffel Tower without its antenna?

9. How many home runs did Cardinal Mark McGwire hit in 1998?

10. Which actor originally played Albus Dumbledore in the Harry Potter films?

a speech. The first way is by orally stating your speech sources during the delivery of your speech and the second is in written form on your outline in the bibliography.

Students often find themselves in trouble when they do not cite the information they have researched in oral or written form. This is called plagiarism. **Plagiarism** is, simply stated, stealing someone else's work. This happens when students copy someone else's work and then present it as their own. We believe that most plagiarism occurs because a student is not sure how to present the information that he or she has gathered: A student either uses the author's exact words without mentioning the source or paraphrases the main ideas without giving credit to the author. You can avoid plagiarism by citing all your sources and indicating when you use any part of someone else's work. This is easy to do.

When citing sources orally within your speech, simply say, "According to (the organization or people who conducted the research), a study done in (give year) found that (your point). If you are in doubt about whether you are plagiarizing, ask your instructor. Never take credit for something that isn't your own work. Since you won't be writing out your speech, you'll need to state all your sources orally during your speech as you present the data you researched.

You will then need to cite your sources in writing on your bibliography by following a standard format. There are several accepted formats, the most common being MLA and APA. Ask your instructor if he or she has a preference. You can find examples for most standard formats by searching for them online. There are also Web sites where you can type information (Title, author, publisher, date, etc.) into the form provided and it is formatted correctly for you. You can then copy and paste the completed list into your bibliography and add the bibliography to your outline. You can also contact your school's writing lab for assistance or consult your library.

Although some speeches draw on your own knowledge, very often that knowledge originated with another source. After all, someone showed you how to change the oil in your car, or you learned how to keyboard from an owner's manual, or your "original" recipe started with a basic one in a cookbook. Giving credit to the original source of your information is necessary to build credibility with your audience and avoid plagiarism.

All the work you have done so far has prepared you to know what you are going to speak about, the people you will be speaking to, the reason for your speech, and what you will say. You may believe that you are ready to present your speech. But, remember, you are not handing the audience a written report. You will be speaking aloud to people who will not only be listening to you but watching you as well. Therefore, you must decide what additional elements you can use to make your speech better and help your audience stay motivated to listen!

How Do I Make My Speech Better?

Beginning speakers often overlook a very important element that can enhance their speeches. **Presentation aids** can help you get your message across to your audience and help you keep their interest. They can also help you with speech anxiety by giving you an additional element on which to focus your energy.

Presentation aids are elements that assist speakers in communicating their message. There are numerous types of aids that can be used to enhance your presentation. A souvenir from your vacation, a video on YouTube, or a PowerPoint presentation can all be used to help speakers enhance their oral message. Your main purpose as a speaker is to deliver specific information to your audience while keeping them interested. Using visual representations or audio clips can help your audience better understand and maintain interest in what you are telling them because it allows them to engage an additional sensory mode. To hear a description of a tarantula is far less powerful than seeing one. You could listen to someone explain jazz, but it is much more exciting to hear a clip of some great New Orleans jazz. You can describe the smell of the ocean on your beach vacation, but adding an air freshener that smells like that breeze would be more enticing. Allowing your audience to use their senses, other than hearing, helps them to experience your message fully.

The first thought that most people have when they think about presentation aids is a poster. Today we have many choices from which we can choose. Let's examine the various types of presentation aids that you might consider using to enhance your speech.

Digital presentations are currently the most frequently used medium for enhancing a speech. Digital presentations use computers, software, and projectors to display information. We are probably all familiar with Microsoft's PowerPoint presentational software. It's difficult to find a college classroom, boardroom, meeting room, or conference center that isn't equipped for digital presentations. It's doubtful that anyone reading this has never seen such a digital presentation, in fact, many of you have probably created one. If such equipment is available to you, use it. No matter what software the program uses (PowerPoint is the most commonly used), you'll find it easy to use for producing a quality visual aid to add to your speech delivery. There are some guidelines for digital presentations to help you create an effective one.

These guidelines should be followed when creating a digital slide or slide show. Many of them can also be applied to any other graphic you are creating, whether digitally or by hand.

1. *Background.*   Choose simple backgrounds that won't compete with your material. Use the same background throughout the presentation.

2. *Color.* Black, blue, and green are the most visible. Avoid purple, brown, pink, and yellow. Use no more than four colors overall in your presentation.

3. *Clutter.* Don't put too much on a slide. Leave empty space, it will be easier for your audience to understand the words and graphics.

4. *Fonts.* Use sans-serif fonts (without the little "hooks") such as Arial or Helvetica, as they are easier on the eyes than serif fonts such as Times New Roman or Palatino. Use an 18- to 24-point font size or larger for headings. Use the same font throughout the text and avoid using all capital letters.

5. *Graphics.* Include pictures in your presentation, but use them for a reason, not just for decoration. Avoid the use of animation. It is distracting. Use simple electronic transitions and be consistent.

6. *Brief.* Keep the text short and simple. Avoid the use of full sentences and use bullet points. Limit the number of slides. No one stays interested in a "never ending" slide show.

7. *Charts and graphs should "speak" alone.* Don't add a lot of words to charts or graphs. Create them wisely and let them "speak for themselves." You can refer to them or offer explanations verbally to help the audience follow them.

8. *Imbed.* Imbed your visuals and audio clips into the slides. It makes your speech flow better and you don't waste time setting up multiple files. They are just a click away—easy to access and easy to follow.

9. *Avoid the familiar.* PowerPoint software is commonly used for digital presentations, so your audience may have already seen the clipart and backgrounds. Try to avoid those that are too common and familiar. If you remember them from another presentation, your audience will too. Incorporate your own visuals whenever possible. This will help keep the audience's interest.

10. *Practice.* Use the presentation while you practice your speech. You can learn when to advance the slides and what you need to say. This will decrease your anxiety and relieve your nerves as you learn how to work through the presentation *before* you give it!

Yes, the old adage one picture is worth a thousand words is correct, particularly when it comes to delivering an effective speech. Adding a **picture** or **video** to your explanation helps your audience understand your material by "seeing" it. Talking about someone? Show us a picture of the person; in fact, if your speech is primarily about one person, place, or thing, show several pictures. Do you have a short video from YouTube or a clip from a movie? Show it to us. Learn how to create a media presentation and incorporate it into an effective slide show. Few other techniques are as effective for your audience as adding an appropriately placed picture to your speech.

What's better than a picture? The **object** itself, if easily portable, beats a picture as a visual aid. Within reason actually bringing the real object for presentation in your speech may be a good option. For example, you could show us a picture of that quilt your grandma made, but actually showing us the quilt would be more effective. Demonstration speeches often require numerous objects to be used as props to show the audience step-by-step how to do something. Actually seeing a procedure is more effective than seeing pictures of it or even a video. The object(s) should be easy to transport and store before and after your speak. Consider its weight and size, and be aware of any policies that are in effect about various objects at the location of your speech. At the community college where we teach, weapons of all kinds are banned from the campus. Consequently, students doing speeches about guns, knives, hunting, or other activities involving a weapon must use a picture or video, even if the real object would be more effective.

You should also consider your audience's "comfort" level with an object. You may be perfectly comfortable handling your pet snake, but will your audience, or instructor, feel at ease with it curling around your arm in the classroom? If the object is too small to be seen by the entire audience then you have two options. If available, you can use a camera that when focused on the object, will project its image onto a screen. If this technology isn't available, your other option is to have enough samples of the object so that one can be handed out to all your audience members at one time. While this certainly isn't practical in many instances, it could be useful and effective with small inexpensive items. In fact, a demonstration speech on how to make an inexpensive and delicious dessert may not be effective unless you have samples for everyone!

As mentioned before, you can describe a sound in your speech, but it may not be as effective as hearing an **audio clip** from a CD or other digital source. While you can certainly quote Martin Luther King Jr. by saying "I have a dream . . . ," think of how much more powerful it would be for your audience if they actually heard his magnificent voice booming that message. Trying to adequately describe the difference between rock and jazz can make your audience's head spin; instead, play the music! Make sure it is ready to be heard with a flip of a switch or stroke of key. It is distracting to watch a speaker stop the flow of the speech to find the right track or file.

A **handout** that provides information related to the speech you have just given us is a useful "takeaway." The audience might like to have a copy of your Angel Food Cake recipe, or a list of useful Web sites providing free coupons. You might want to pass out copies of a chart you referred to during your speech. If you are using a handout during your speech, don't pass it out until you want everyone to look at it. Otherwise it can become a distraction. If the handout is to be taken away, then it is best to pass it out at the end of your speech, unless you want the audience to refer to it during various segments of your speech. However, you should never pass around a single object to the class while speaking. It can be distracting, and it decreases the audience's ability to focus on you and your speech.

If you are presenting your speech in an environment that has a **blackboard** or **whiteboard** (think classroom), you can use the board to make quick drawings or charts. Notice the word "quick" in that statement. The board should only be used for simple diagrams or examples that are not highly detailed. If you have graphs and charts, lists, or other more detailed visual elements, prepare them in advance, using some other medium, otherwise you risk the chance of looking unprofessional.

Now that we have discussed the various types of presentation aids you can use to enhance your presentation, we will discuss some additional things you should consider. Presentation aids are designed to add interest to your speech so they should be brief and manageable. You should properly place them in the appropriate section of your speech and then remove them when they no longer apply. You should use them but not abuse them. Do not "talk" to the aid by facing it; you must still face your audience. Never deliver your speech with your back to your audience. Follow these simple rules, and your aids will enhance your speech and add interest for your audience. Once you have created your presentation aids you have completed step 6.

Conclusion

Let's face it: If you want to do something well, you need to dedicate an appropriate amount of time to preparation. An effective speech requires time to prepare. Even though the body of your speech will use most of your speaking time, the introduction and conclusion are extremely important and must be carefully developed. *Outlining* is the process used to achieve the goal of speech organization, step 4 of the nine-step process. The outline provides a map to guide you to finding facts to support your main ideas for your speech. This is done through the process of research.

Researching is step 5 of the nine-step process. You can be better prepared and use your time more effectively by making a research plan. Remember the sources you choose to support your speech topic need to be credible and reliable. You can ensure they are by using the ABCD method and checklist. It's not hard to find sources for your topic. The trick is to locate the sources that are "just right" for your speech. Beginning speakers often overlook a very important element that can enhance their speeches. Presentation aids are elements that assist speakers in communicating their message. There are numerous types of *presentation aids* that can be used to enhance your speech. Once your presentation aids have been incorporated into your speech, you have completed step 6 of the nine-step process.

■ DISCUSSION QUESTIONS

1. What are the parts of an effective introduction? Why are they necessary?
2. What is the difference between a working outline and a formal outline?
3. Choose a topic and list several sources you could use that you already know exist.
4. What considerations should you use when choosing sources to support your topic?
5. Why do you need to use the ABCD model to check the credibility of your sources, especially those found on the Internet?
6. What are the advantages of using presentation aids?
7. Choose a speech topic and list several aids you could use to enhance the speech. Why did you choose those particular aids?

■ KEY WORDS

audio clip
authority
bias
bibliography
blackboard
causal organization
chronological organization
conclusion
content
credibility
currency
design
digital presentations
formal outline
grabber
handout
Internet
Internet address
interview
introduction
media

object
organizational patterns
outlining
personal experience
picture
plagiarism
presentation aids
preview
priority organization
problem solution organization
process organization
research
research plan
spatial organization
speaking outline
specific topic
surveys
vidco
whiteboard
WIFM
working outline

From Beginning To End

?At What Time

Throughout?

WHEN?

During Which Time

?Meanwhile?

THE COURSE OF

When?

. . . to create speech notes . . .
. . . to practice . . .
. . . to deliver your speech . . .
. . . step 7 . . . step 8 . . . step 9 . . .

- When Do I Use Notes?
- When Do I Practice?
- When Do I Deliver?
- When Do I Use Verbal Elements?
- When Do I Use Nonverbal Elements?
- When Do I Answer Questions?

Now that you have an outline and have chosen presentation aids to enhance your speech, you should begin preparing the notes you will use for practice and then refine those notes for use when you deliver your speech. This may be the first of several sets of **speech notes** that you will prepare, as you are likely to adjust them each time you practice. Strive for improvement during each practice session and make adjustments to your notes each time. The final notes you take with you to the podium are very important. This is step 7 of the nine-step process.

When Do I Use Notes?

The purpose of podium notes is to allow you to view your points at a glance. Too much writing makes it difficult to focus on your main points. Many speakers choose to use their outline as their podium notes. In fact, this is the choice of most professional speakers as well as your authors when they lecture.

Your notes are personal and should work for you. Make the notes simple and brief. Use the medium that you are the most comfortable with, but keep in mind that the typical 3 × 5 note card is rather small to use for speech notes, as they do not allow you to quickly glance at your notes without losing your train of thought. Keep in mind that several sheets of paper may rustle if not bound together by a paperclip, staple, or binder. Whatever "paper" you use, you do not want it to become a distraction to your audience.

Be sure to have your notes in the proper order and, if they aren't bound, number the cards or pages to keep them sequential. Make sure they are neat and legible. Don't try to fit everything on just one or two note cards. Notes are your lifeline if your thoughts fail at the podium. Guard them—they are priceless! Once you have your podium notes compiled, it is time to use them to practice your speech.

When Do I Practice?

The old saying "**Practice** makes perfect" is certainly applicable to public speaking. Practicing is the eighth step of the process. You can gain valuable insight from practicing that will provide you with the information you need to make adjustments to your speech before you present it to your audience. Practice giving your speech to another person, use a recorder or your smart phone, or watch yourself in a full-length mirror. Practicing in front of friends or family is also valuable. By doing one or all of these things, several times, you can find out how you will look and sound to your audience, and you can add or delete items from your notes as is necessary.

Although you won't know exactly what you will do at the podium when you actually deliver your speech, practicing it in advance will reveal if any adjustments need to be made. Practicing can also help you determine how long your presentation will take to deliver. Through practice you can gain mastery over your volume, pitch, and speaking rate, as well as the time element of your speech. You can discover if you overuse "um" and "uh." You will learn about your eye contact, gesturing, and appearance. You can practice using your presentation aids. Be sure to note any adjustments that are needed and add these items to your final notes. Without rehearsal, your speech won't be effective—practice is important.

When Do I Deliver?

This is what it has all been leading up to. It's your time to shine at the podium. All the hard work of focusing, researching, and organizing has prepared you, and you have put the finishing touches on your speech. Now get ready to stand and deliver! **Delivery** is the process of presenting your speech to an audience and is the ninth and final step of the nine-step process. It is accomplished through the use of verbal and nonverbal elements of communication. Language, or the words you say, are the verbal elements of delivery. Anything that is not language, such as facial expressions and gestures, are examples of nonverbal elements of delivery. All of these factors have a significant impact on the effectiveness of your speech.

You may believe the information you have gathered to share with your audience is the most important part of your speech. Certainly the content is a major factor in how effectively you will communicate with your audience. However, the way you deliver your message is equally important. In fact, without an effective delivery, your audience may drift off. They may never listen to the information you have spent so much time researching and organizing. This makes delivery a key factor in becoming an effective communicator. Your delivery must complement and reinforce the content of your message. There are four ways that speeches can be delivered. The type of delivery you choose is a key factor in determining whether or not your audience stays focused on your message.

Impromptu

An **impromptu delivery** is the most common type of speech delivery. It is the act of giving a spontaneous, unprepared speech without prior notice. This is the kind of speaking we engage in daily. Someone stops us and asks directions. Our boss surprises us with an award at a corporate dinner and asks us to "say a few words." The person who is supposed to introduce your luncheon speaker isn't coming so you have to do the introduction. You are leaving for the weekend and your spouse needs to know the kids' schedule while you are gone. All of these are examples of speeches that use impromptu delivery.

There are lots of advantages to becoming an effective impromptu speaker. Since it is the type of communication we use most frequently, the better we do it the easier it will be for us to get our message across. Most speech teachers, including us, hope their students will become better impromptu speakers, thus improving their overall communication.

However, there are disadvantages to impromptu speaking as well. First and foremost, there is no time to prepare. How many of us have experienced a situation where we wish we hadn't said what we did? The best way to become a more effective impromptu speaker is to learn the basics. Having time to prepare, organize, and practice other speeches will more readily prepare you for situations when you have to think and speak "on your feet." Completing a formal public speaking class is one way to achieve that goal.

Manuscript

If you have ever seen a televised presidential address, you've seen a **manuscript delivery.** Put simply, a manuscript delivery is when the speaker reads the words, either from a paper text or off a teleprompter. This form of delivery is usually the least effective style in most speaking situations. Reading causes a speaker to avoid looking at the audience and it also causes him or her to forget to use gestures. Speaking from a manuscript should only be used in very specific situations. If you are going to be extensively quoted and it is vitally important that you be able to defend exactly what you said (think government/politics), then you might consider a manuscript delivery. In all other situations, avoid choosing this style. Most audiences consider speakers who read to them as boring.

Memorized

Our experience in the public speaking classroom has shown that students often choose a **memorized delivery,** since they are not allowed to read their speech to the audience. Memorized speeches are rarely effective due to the unreliability of memory. We often forget what comes next, confusing ourselves and our audience while we frown and try to remember the next sentence. When we recite from memory, our voice adopts a different rhythm than our normal speech pattern—one which is often annoying to the audience. There are situations where memorization is appropriate, such as when acting, but usually it is a good idea to avoid this type of delivery for a speech, for no other reason than its unreliability.

Extemporaneous

Extemporaneous delivery refers to giving a speech that is prepared and practiced, yet not memorized. This is the most versatile of all four delivery styles. This delivery style overcomes the disadvantages of the other three styles by allowing the speaker to use notes or an outline. The speaker feels more comfortable with speaking, having already practiced using his or her notes. This delivery style doesn't require memorizing the material or speaking on the spur of the moment. This results in a more "personal" delivery to the audience. The speaker is free to make eye contact and to react to audience feedback. Vocal tones and gestures seem natural and the audience feels like the speaker is having a conversation with them. This style of delivery is the one used by effective public speakers.

Once you know which style of delivery you should use, you need to think about the delivery elements you will use to give your speech. Delivery elements fall into two categories: verbal elements and nonverbal elements. We'll first focus on those elements of your presentation that deal with the words you will use during your delivery. The words you speak and how you say them can help you establish a rapport with your audience and help you efficiently convey your message.

When Do I Use Verbal Elements?

One way that we can send a message to others is through the use of **verbal elements.** This form of communication uses **language,** a written or spoken system of symbols (words) to convey a message. How we use language greatly affects the delivery of our speech.

Language

A smooth delivery depends partly on the words you use. Speakers must be aware of how they arrange words so that the audience will perceive the intended meaning. This aspect of language is called **semantics,** the meaning of words. Just because everyone in your audience may speak or understand English does not guarantee that they will understand what you are saying.

Words are symbolic. They describe the mental images that we encode in our head (unit 1). Your audience members will *individually* decode your spoken message and create their own mental image from your words. For example, if you say you have three dogs, your audience will envision a range of critters, from poodles to retrievers. How can you be sure that the audience understands that you are talking about German shepherds? Even if you use the dictionary definition of a word, you cannot be sure everyone will know what you mean. Dictionaries carry several definitions for any one word. It is your duty, as a speaker, to make sure your audience understands your intended meaning. Avoid using slang in your speech and define any technical terms you may be using. Choose precise and descriptive terms, but don't choose words that are over your listeners' heads, or they won't understand what you're saying. Conversely, choosing words that your audience may feel are simplistic implies they are idiots. You don't want to have a defensive audience!

Choose your words carefully. Think about the message you are trying to deliver to your specific audience. Your previous preparation and audience analysis can help you target your information to your audience and give you insight as to what language is appropriate for the particular group to which you are speaking.

Grammar

A discussion on language would not be complete without considering grammar. **Grammar** is the system of word structure and arrangement for the language you are speaking. Standard grammar is very important. You would not walk into a room and say, "You, morning how are good?" and expect anyone to understand you. Rather, you would say, "Good morning, how are you?" Those rules and skills you learned in your English classes will pay off nicely in the realm of public speaking. Remember that speech delivery should occur as a formalized presentation, and therefore formal Standard English should be used.

All languages have dialects, or words and phrases that are commonly used and accepted by people who live in a specific geographic region. For example, the phrases "I seen" and "I come" might be used as the past tense of see and come more frequently in some sections of the United States instead of the grammatically correct "I saw" and "I came." While phrases such as these may be understandable or acceptable to some audiences, they are not grammatically correct and should not be used when delivering your speech. Using proper grammar, such as the right verb tense—past, present, or future—and speaking in complete sentences will enhance your delivery and the ultimate outcome of your speech.

Remember, most of us don't typically speak formal English on a day-to-day basis; therefore, we may need to think about what pronouns to use. For example, the proper order for the subjects of a sentence are: "My friends and I," not "Me and my friends." Make sure your subjects and your verbs agree. Use of Standard English conveys credibility and is one way to establish your authority as a speaker. The point is to make sure your grammar doesn't hinder your speech. If the audience starts becoming distracted by your use of improper grammar, they aren't likely to see you as an authority to whom they should listen.

Transitions

One of your responsibilities as a speaker is to help the audience understand your ideas. You need to lead your audience as you shift from one idea to another so they won't become lost. Shifting from one point to another is called making a **transition.** Transitions are used when you are moving to another subject, much like moving to another paragraph in your textbook. Often, beginning speakers fall into the trap of using the same transition word over and over, such as *and, but,* or *then.* In moving from one point to another, you can use other connecting phrases, many of which will enhance the relationship of the elements in your speech. We have provided you with a list of sample transitions that can be used to shift your speech from one point to another during your delivery.

Sample Transitions

on the other hand	in comparison
in addition	for example
in other words	furthermore
however	another reason
we might overlook	some think
first, second . . .	I suggest
as a result	consequently

A good way to help you break out of the *and* trap is to write more creative transition words and phrases in the margins of your notes. Then at the podium you can quickly glance at these transition cues to help you move smoothly and meaningfully from one segment of your speech to another.

Articulation

If your audience can't understand what you are saying because you mumble or run your words together, you aren't going to keep their attention. **Articulation,** the process of emitting clear individual sounds that form distinct words, is a skill that needs to be mastered quickly for effective delivery. There are two considerations when practicing clear articulation. First you must make sure you are saying the words correctly, which is **pronunciation,** separating and accenting the syllables in the correct manner. Once you are sure of how a word should be pronounced, the actual act of pronouncing the individual vowel and consonant sounds is called **enunciation.** If your diction is clear, your words will probably be properly enunciated. If you have an individual concern or problem in this area, your instructor can help you.

Speakers who aren't concerned about both pronunciation and enunciation make an audience member's job very difficult! Since your listeners decide the meaning of the words you are using, correct pronunciation keeps them on track with your line of thinking. If you are using difficult or technical words, check with an authority in this area for the correct pronunciation, or at least look the words up in the dictionary. Even better, find the word in an online dictionary with audio clips so you can actually "hear" the correct pronunciation. Inevitably, if you don't, someone in your audience will be familiar with the word and realize you have made a mistake. What if you are persuading people to vote for you for student senate, and the one person who realizes that you mispronounced a word is the deciding vote? At the very least, it can be embarrassing, and that only adds to speech anxiety, which is certainly something you want to avoid. Better to check before you give your speech, than to be sorry later. Following is a list of commonly mispronounced words.

Commonly Mispronounced Words

aluminum (ah-loom-in-um)	epitome (i-PIT-o-mee)
anonymous (ah-NON-uh-muss)	escape (es-KAPE)
athlete (ATH-leet)	et cetera (et-SET-er-a)
athletics (ath-LET-iks)	facade (fah-SOD)
autopsy (AW-top-see)	faux pas (FO-PAH)
banquet (BAN-kuit)	fungi (FUN-GUY)
Beethoven (BAY-toe-vin)	genuine (JEN-u-in)
blase (blah-zay)	heir (air)
brochure (bro-SHUR)	homage (OHM-aj)
cache (kash)	hysteria (hi-STARE-ee-ah)
chagrin (sha-GRIN)	impotent (IMP-o-tent)
chasm (KA-zum)	indict (in-DITE)
chef (shef)	infamous (IN-fa-muss)

(Continued)

chic (sheek)	Italian (it-AL-ee-in)
Chopin (SHO-pan)	lingerie (LON-jer-ay)
comparable (KOM-pra-bull)	mischievous (MISS-chi-vuss)
disastrous (diz-AA-struss)	often (OFF-en)
drama (DRAH-ma)	picture (PICK-shur)
electoral (eh-LEC-tore-all)	pitcher (PIT-chure)
elite (ee-LEET)	poignant (POYN-yant)
police (poe-LEESS)	subtle (SUH-till)
precocious (pre-KO-shuss)	sword (sord)
preferable (PREFF-er-a-bull)	theater (THEE-e-ter)
probably (PRAH-bab-lee)	vehement (VEE-a-mint)
recognize (REH-cog-nize)	virile (VEER-ill)
statistics (sta-TI-sticks)	Worcestershire (WUSS-ter-sure)

There are probably many more words that could be added to this list. However, the important issue is that if you are not sure how a word is pronounced, find out!

Fillers

We've discussed choosing our words carefully to get our message across and keep the audience listening. Now we need to take a look at words (and sounds) that we want to avoid when presenting our speech. Inexperienced speakers frequently use **fillers,** such as "um," "ah," "you know," "like," and others, that are ineffective. Time fillers make you appear hesitant and unprepared. If they're used frequently, audience members may begin counting them rather than listening to your speech.

We use fillers because our minds work faster than our mouths. A simple cure for fillers is to close your mouth. If your mouth is closed while you are mentally catching up you can't "um" or "ah." Use of "you know" and "like" is considered slang in a formal presentation. They, too, should be avoided. It is fair to say that most speakers are unaware of the fillers they use. However ignorance doesn't change the fact that repetitive fillers are annoying when heard during a speech delivery.

Vocals

When you are speaking aloud the sounds produced by your voice convey a message. As a speaker, you depend on your voice. The sound of your voice is produced by air that has been stored in your lungs. The capacity of the lungs is determined by a muscle located under the lungs and rib cage. This muscle is called the **diaphragm.** Like other muscles in your body, the diaphragm will tense as you become nervous. This tension causes the muscle to shrink, diminishing the potential air supply of your lungs. Air (as breath) is the primary source of the sounds we make, or our **vocals.**

To produce sounds successfully, we must know how to regulate and control this flow of air. Breathing normally requires no conscious control or awareness. It is an automatic response of our body, one that keeps us alive. However, if we add the element of speaking, we must consciously control the breathing process to produce effective, pleasing vocal tones. Air from the lungs will pass through the windpipe and into the **larynx,** which contains the membranes known as the vocal cords. As this air passes over the larynx, sounds called tones are produced. The mouth then concentrates these tones into words. The cavity of the sinuses and the head provide chambers to further refine and enhance the sound as it leaves your body, thus creating what others hear as your voice. The voice must be used effectively in order to have variety and clarity in your speech. Breathing correctly and using air to mold the sounds of your voice when speaking is an important factor in effective delivery.

The Voice

How you use your **voice** affects the verbal delivery of your speech. **Fluidity** is the ease and smoothness of the verbal delivery. While a singsong cadence isn't the most effective way to deliver a speech, neither is a choppy delivery full of unnecessary pauses. Practicing out loud will help you feel comfortable with what you are saying and help with the fluidity of your voice and speech, making it more appealing to your audience. **Tone** is important as well and consists of three elements: rate, volume, and pitch. These elements, when used together, create vocal sounds. **Rate** is the speed at which your words are actually delivered. Most people speak at a rate of approximately 200–250 words per minute. Speakers often increase the rate at which they are speaking when they become nervous or caught up in their speech. If a speaker speaks too quickly the audience can't understand him or her. However, effective use of rate, both speeding up and slowing down, can create interest for your audience. **Pitch** refers to the range of your voice, or where a sound you make would be placed on a musical scale. Although we don't normally think of the spoken word as musical, all sounds we create can be evaluated for relative "highness" or "lowness." This range of sound creates the pitch of your voice. While deep, low voices are often considered interesting and attractive, high-pitched sounds are considered screechy and annoying. When we become nervous or excited the pitch of our voice often rises, possibly reducing our audience's desire to listen. **Volume** refers to the softness or loudness of the tones produced when sound resonates in our sinus cavities. Although we have some control over the volume of our voice, some people have voices that are naturally loud, and others may speak louder than they need to due to physical challenges such as hearing impairment. To be an effective public speaker we need to project loudly enough to be heard by those in the last row, without blasting out those sitting in the front.

Pauses, the time in between sounds, are also a factor in vocal delivery. Placing short pauses in your speech can be an effective way to emphasize important points. However, they should not be overused nor should they last for more than a few seconds. Unintentional pauses caused by a lapse in memory can be a problem. Don't panic; the audience probably won't even notice if you don't fill the pause with unnecessary fillers. However, if you experience a lot of pauses during practice, you probably need to practice your speech more. Numerous pauses are received by the audience as lack of preparation. This could result in a loss of credibility and ultimately your audience's attention.

Effective speakers utilize all of the verbal elements to create interest for their speech. However, like any other form of communication, when misused they can annoy your audience. Remember, the language you use can put your audience at ease or scare them away! Preparation and practice are the stepping stones to effective verbal delivery.

Vocal Exercises

To appreciate more fully the membrane called the diaphragm, get an ordinary balloon. Uninflated, the balloon's texture resembles the diaphragm itself without speech anxiety; it is resilient and pliable, yet remarkably strong (unless attacked with a pin or sharp object). (Remember that this membrane lies beneath the lungs and controls the volume of air permitted in the lungs.) Now blow up the balloon. As you perform this simple task of transferring air from your lungs to the balloon, notice how often you need to take a new breath to blow. Does the exchange of air in your lungs (i.e., inhaling and exhaling) take five to seven seconds or longer? Or are you more rapidly blowing up the balloon? The shorter the time for a complete breath (inhaling and exhaling), the shallower your breath, and the less lung capacity or potential capacity you are using. The inflated balloon resembles the texture of the diaphragm with speech anxiety—not too much give. With this exercise you have seen two things: the texture of the diaphragm and the capacity of your lungs.

Because air (in the form of breath) is the primary source of the sounds we make, let's look at the breathing process. To produce sounds successfully, we must know how to regulate and control the air flow. Here's the process. When we breathe, the following physical actions occur:

1. The muscles of the diaphragm tense, contract, and move downward, becoming more flat than domed.
2. This descending movement of the diaphragm compresses the stomach, liver, and kidneys, which causes a bulge in the abdominal walls.
3. The rib cage rises up and outward.

The preceding procedure causes the air pressure in the lungs to decrease, creating a partial vacuum so that air from outside rushes in to equalize the pressure.

As we reverse the process and exhale, the procedure reverses itself.

1. Relaxation of muscles allows the diaphragm to move upward (or we constrict the diaphragm, forcing air out of the lungs).
2. The stomach, liver, and kidneys return to their uncompressed positions.
3. The ribs then move down and inward due to the pull of gravity.

All of the above actions cause a decrease in the size of the chest cavity, which compresses the air in the lungs. This means that the air pressure in the lungs is now greater than the pressure outside the body and air is expelled through the mouth and nose.

In the absence of any physical respiratory problems, breathing (inhaling and exhaling) requires no conscious control or awareness. It is an automatic response of our body that keeps us alive. However, when we talk, we must be aware of what we are doing in order to control the breathing process consciously and produce effective, pleasing vocal tones.

When proper breathing techniques are used, the speaker inhales less frequently and will not have to gasp for breath because there will be a reserve of air. Longer phrases can be uttered, and jerky rhythms can be avoided. Furthermore, the larynx and throat will be less tense, which will improve vocal quality.

Practice the breathing techniques in the four "Strengthen Your Skills" exercises on the following page. With practice over time, you should notice an improvement in your breathing, resulting in a smooth, relaxed, and efficient speech delivery.

Strengthen Your Skills

Breathing Exercise

Purpose: The purpose of this exercise is to correct shallow breathing, which can interfere with effective speech.

Procedure:

1. Lie with your back flat on the floor. Place a book or pillow under your head, which will raise your head three-fourths to one inch. This places your head in the proper position for normal breathing.

2. Put your right hand on your abdomen and your left hand on the upper part of your chest above your sternum. Breathe as naturally as possible; inhale through your nose and exhale through your mouth or nose. Notice the expansion and contraction that occurs under your right hand and the little movement under your left hand. When you are aware of these movements, stand up and breathe in the same manner. Be careful not to lift your shoulders.

Strengthen Your Skills

Yawning Exercise

Purpose: The purpose of this exercise is to feel the relaxation in the throat that will keep the voice from sounding tense.

Procedure:

1. Rest your tongue on the floor of your mouth and yawn.

2. Repeat several times. This will result in a reasonably relaxed throat.

3. Say "ah," continuing the sound for about five seconds. Don't let any tightness or tension enter your throat. If your throat begins to tense, discontinue the sound and repeat the yawn before attempting to vocalize again.

4. When you can sustain the sound for five seconds or more without tension, try the exercise by vocalizing each of the following sounds: "oo," "ee," "uh," "ou," "oh."

Strengthen Your Skills

Alphabet Exercise

Purpose: The purpose of this exercise is to allow you to determine if your voice support is sufficient or if air is escaping unnecessarily.

Procedure:
1. Take a deep breath.

2. Without hurrying too much, try to say the alphabet in one breath. If you can't make it all the way through, you aren't breathing correctly. Don't strain. Relax. Easy does it.

Strengthen Your Skills

Loudness Exercise

Purpose: The purpose of this exercise is to increase your volume by learning how to avoid excess air release.

Procedure:
1. Whisper the sound "ah."

2. Repeat the sound as you gradually build the volume, but avoid breathiness. Remember to breathe deeply and tense those inner throat muscles to keep the unvoiced airflow from leaking out.

When Do I Use Nonverbal Elements?

While there are several verbal elements that we've explored, we still need to consider another group of factors. Elements that are not specifically related to language can also enhance what you say to your audience. **Nonverbal elements** are exactly what the word implies, not verbal. Simply put, they are *not* language. These elements are significant factors in how we convey messages. Many of our nonverbal behaviors are expressed without a conscious decision to communicate, and they are often interpreted by others differently than how we intend. This makes thinking about and practicing them as a part of your speech delivery important to the out-come of your speech.

Appearance

Your overall **appearance** can affect how your speech is accepted by your audience. First impressions are often lasting impressions. The way the mem-bers of your audience initially perceive you will affect how they respond to you. Your appearance can also affect your credibility. Presenting the best image you can is important. The speaker should be aware of the usual "dress code" of the audience. Will the audience be dressed casually or formally? As the speaker, you will want to conform to the audience's standard. You would not want to wear shorts and a tank top to give a speech to an audi-ence dressed in business suits. You would probably not get past the guards at the gate! Keep this in mind on the day you are to present speeches in your classroom as well. Do not dress differently than you normally do for class, unless you are using a gimmick or using your clothes as a visual aid. Dress-ing up on presentation day may cause your audience to wonder why you have on a suit or dress when you normally wear jeans and a T-shirt. This will detract from, rather than aid, your delivery, unless your clothing is part of your speech. In some cases, clothing can be a dramatic element used to convey a mood to your audience. If you were speaking about the history of the 1960s, you might dress in a tie-dyed T-shirt, wear a headband, and wear a peace-sign necklace. If you are speaking about donating blood, you might wear a Red Cross t-shirt or dress as Dracula (which one student actually did). These details can add pizzazz to your speech and help your audience get interested in what you have to say.

Avoid anything in your attire that might distract the audience from focusing on you. T-shirts with logos or graphics that don't relate to your topic, ball caps that shade your eyes, and hairstyles that cover your face and cause you to flick your hair are all things to avoid. We also recom-mend that you wear comfortable clothes. The day you deliver your speech is not the day you want to wear new shoes. You are trying to concentrate on what you are saying and do not need any uncomfortable distractions.

Facial Expressions

Your face is a valuable asset to your delivery. Your **facial expressions,** or the animation of your features, allow you to convey emotion without the use of any words. We let our faces tell a story just as much as our language does. However, when you approach the podium to give your speech, you do not want to show you are nervous by wearing an expressionless stone mask. This physical reaction to fear will severely limit your ability to tell your story. Your audience will be watching your facial expressions. If you can show you are interested in your topic through your facial expressions, your audience will become interested as well. Animated use of the face will cue your audience that you are sincere and will serve as an invitation for them to join in your message, thus also helping you to relax.

Eye Contact

Many of you probably have heard the expression that the eyes are the windows to the soul. The eyes truly are the most important aspect of the face, and making **eye contact** with another person—looking directly at him or her—conveys a wealth of emotion and communication to that person—a sense of sincerity that does not occur when looking at the wall, at notes, or over the heads of listeners. Looking at all members in the audience individually at some point during your speech is wise, even if this means you are able to look at each one only briefly. You can shift your gaze from one member to another throughout your entire speech. For a few moments, each audience member will feel like you are speaking directly to him or her. Do not look at your listener's forehead, do not look at his or her arm; look directly into his or her eyes. Look at all eyes in the room. Looking at people invites, almost commands, them to look back at you and pay attention. When they look and pay attention, they are listening. The best procedure is to maintain frequent eye contact with as many members of your audience as possible.

Posture

The manner in which you hold your body is known as **posture.** Good posture, (remember when your mother told you to stand up straight and not slouch?) is very useful in public speaking. Most likely, your instructor will ask you to use a podium or lectern when you speak. It will be important to place your notes on this device and stand directly behind it, straight and tall. Do not lean on or over the podium. Leaning over the podium suggests sloppiness and insincerity to your audience, and leaning on the podium could cause you to push it directly off of its stand! On the other hand, you don't want to hold yourself in a stiff or rigid position either. Standing up straight and tall should look natural, not forced. To take a comfortable stance, place your feet directly below your shoulders and distribute your weight evenly. By doing this you will avoid any unnecessary movements that often accompany nervousness, such as shifting your weight from foot to foot, or swaying side to side or back and forth.

Gestures

The movements of the hand(s) or body to add emphasis to important points are known as **gestures.** Most of us use our hands a great deal in informal speaking, but this is one of the least used tactics by beginning speakers. If we are trying to give directions to a friend, we often point and raise our arms to indicate the direction in which we want our friend to turn. When some speakers get up to the podium, they grip the sides of it until their knuckles turn white, clasp their hands behind their back, jangle the change in their pocket, or drum their fingers on the podium. In doing this, they ignore the valuable everyday habit of using gestures to emphasize or complement what they are saying.

Movement attracts attention, and gestures can be used in a positive way to get that attention when you need it the most. There are hundreds of gestures available to you as a speaker, but be careful not to overuse them. Remember that gestures can be used to add emphasis, but you certainly don't want every word or sentence in your speech emphasized. Furthermore, you want to be sure that no gestures you use convey obscene or inappropriate meanings to your audience.

You can also gesture with your body. A quick step back from the podium might emphasize a message of caution or alarm. However, although gesturing is important, too much movement can distract audience members. They will pay attention to your movements and not to what you are saying. Moving away from the podium can cause you to lose the interest of your audience as well, and should only be done for emphasis, unless you are giving a lecture. Notes should always remain on the podium and not be carried or held. Moving toward your audience implies informality and is not the normal posture for public speaking. Use your movements appropriately. Don't be stiff but don't move so frequently that your audience suffers motion sickness from watching you.

Strengthen Your Skills

Tell Them Where You Parked

Purpose: The purpose of this exercise is to show you the importance and natural use of gestures by trying to avoid their use.

Procedure:

1. Stand behind the podium and clasp your hands behind your back.

2. Using no hand gestures, give directions from where you are standing to your parked car.

3. Does this seem awkward and strange? It should, because gestures are very commonly used by all of us.

Now that we know which nonverbal elements we can incorporate into our delivery, the final item we must deal with occurs after the delivery is over—questions! It is important to prepare for questions from your audience.

When Do I Answer Questions?

While your public speaking class may not include time for questions from your audience after your speech, a question-and-answer period is often a standard feature of many speaking engagements. In order to help you prepare for these situations, we'll offer some suggestions for making them go as smoothly as possible.

1. Be prepared. You need to know a speech topic better than an essay topic. Think about the type of questions you might be asked and prepare a response to them.

2. Repeat questions to make sure everyone in the audience knows what you are responding to before you give your answer.

3. Give straightforward, concise answers. This is not a discussion period. Allow only one follow-up question per person (if requested) and move on. You want to answer as many questions as you can in the time allowed.

4. If you don't understand the question, say, "Here's what I think the question is [fill in with your perception]. Is that correct?" If you don't know the answer, say so, don't try and fake it.

5. Even if you perceive a question as hostile, don't react to it that way. Never use sarcasm or any other tone that may be interpreted by your audience as negative. You as the speaker can control the situation by not allowing yourself to be manipulated.

Conclusion

The actual delivery of your speech depends on preparation and practice. You will need to approach the podium with your final speech notes, prepared in step 7, and know you can do a good job. Using these notes, and making adjustments to them during practice, step 8, can make your speech nearly perfect. We have discussed numerous elements that are very important for your speech to be effective, but it is the verbal and nonverbal elements of your delivery that ultimately convey your message to your audience. Everything you do at the podium sends a message. Paying attention to these elements when you practice your speech will result in a speech that is more effective when you actually deliver it, step 9 and will engage the audience while you convey your message

■ **DISCUSSION QUESTIONS**

1. Why are your final notes so important?
2. Why is practicing your speech important for an effective delivery?
3. Why is it important to practice your speech out loud?
4. What should you look or listen for when practicing your speech?
5. Discuss how rate, volume, and pitch combine to create the tone of your voice.
6. Why are the verbal and nonverbal elements of delivery as important as the content of your speech?

KEY WORDS

appearance
articulation
delivery
diaphragm
enunciation
extemporaneous delivery
eye contact
facial expressions
fillers
fluidity
gestures
grammar
impromptu delivery
language
larynx
manuscript delivery

memorized delivery
nonverbal elements
pauses
pitch
posture
practice
pronunciation
rate
semantics
speech notes
tone
transitions
verbal elements
vocals
voice
volume

Locality ? Region

? Position Spot

Section Venue

WHERE?

POINT LOCATION

SCENE ?

Site Locale Sector

Where?

. . . applying the nine-step speech process . . .

- Where Do I Speak? . . . in situations requiring information . . .
- Where Do I Speak? . . . in situations requiring persuasion . . .
- Where Do I Speak? . . . in situations requiring celebrations . . .

Now that you have learned the nine-step process for preparing an effective speech, it is time to apply it to create any type of speech that will be podium ready. In our Unit 1 discussion of *why* we study communication, we learned that early Greek citizens gathered to receive or give information, or were called on to debate or vote on a governmental issue, and sometimes were expected to attend special events. These early Greek traditions provided the framework for events where people were speaking to inform, speaking to persuade, and speaking for special occasions—the three speaking categories we still use in modern-day public speaking. We have devoted the first five units of this text to helping you learn the nine-step speech preparation process. This process can now be used as an effective technique for developing a speech in any of these three speaking categories. We will start with applying the nine-step process to create an informative speech.

Situations Requiring Information

You will find many instances of **informative speeches** in your daily life. Did your father give you a list of items to do and reasons why the items needed to be done? Did you inform your

127

roommates what to do before your guests arrive for your party? Did your manager explain what you needed to accomplish during your shift? Were you asked to explain safety procedures to new employees when using the fryers at work? All of these situations in our daily lives require us to either give or listen to information.

The main purpose of the informative speech is to transfer knowledge from speaker to audience. This requires you, as the speaker, to know your subject in detail. Your ability to give effective informative speeches is one of the most important skills you will ever learn, and it will be used both in your career and in your personal life. It is not an exaggeration to state that personal and professional success depends on the effective delivery of facts and knowledge to others.

Categories of Informative Speeches

While the general purpose remains the same for all informative speaking situations, the direction and style in which the information is presented can fall into four different speaking categories: descriptive, demonstration, explanatory, and definitional.

Descriptive Speeches

The **descriptive speech** is used when the speaker wants to use words to provide a clear picture of a person, place, or thing. In descriptive speaking your purpose is to enlighten your audience by describing your subject in detail. Description is effective only when the language chosen is very specific and graphic. For example, notice the difference in the following two descriptions:

"The sky was blue and pink."

"The sky was cotton-candy blue intertwined with an array of swirling pink hues."

Examples that require the use of several of the senses provide a highly effective mental image for your audience. The descriptive speech works well when you want your audience to have a vivid impression or "picture" of the person, place, or thing about which you are speaking. They are also the type of informative speech best used when you want to "transport" your audience to another place or time. Examples of descriptive speeches could include: informing the audience about the effects of sun tanning by describing the process of tanning animal hides, or providing an example of what it is like to be hearing impaired to a hearing audience, or creating an impression of the sensory excitement you felt the first time you viewed the ocean and smelled the salt water! Descriptive speeches are most effective when you enhance your description with presentation aids that further appeal to your audience's senses.

Suggestions to Create a Descriptive Speech

- What makes the person or object unique? Characteristics, functions, or fine points?

- What emotional responses does the topic stir in you? Sadness, anger, joy, or excitement?

- What adjectives best apply to the subject? Large, small, unique, beautiful?

- What are the physical characteristics of the object? Color, smell, shape, taste, sound?

Demonstration Speeches

The **demonstration speech** attempts to show the steps necessary to take a process from beginning to end. This speech shows how something is done or made, how something works, or how something happens. Your goal in this type of speaking is to present the process in a clear, comprehensive, sequential order that your audience can understand and follow while you are speaking. The most effective demonstrations use many visual aids to show step-by-step (with verbal instructions) how something is done. This type of informative speech explains step by step directions on processes (how to make brownies), procedures (how to put out a grease fire), applications (how to use new software) and actions (how a bill becomes a law). These types of speeches offer the audience the best opportunity to actually learn how to do something.

Suggestions to Create a Demonstration Speech

- Cover the entire process from beginning to end.

- Make it visual, but keep safety in mind.

- Have "props" ready and usable.

- Use verbal transitions to lead from point to point.

- Don't skip any steps.

Explanatory Speeches

The **explanatory speech** attempts to provide a clear explanation of a complex issue or idea. These speeches work well for subjects that your audience is not very knowledgeable about or topics that your audience finds confusing. Explanatory speeches connect the topic to other related subjects to create deeper understanding. For example, to explain what Americans refer to as "freedom of speech," you would have to explain the first amendment and its purpose, as well as the historical context that lead to its inclusion in the Constitution. You may be a computer whiz in a class full of people who are computer illiterate. In this case, you are the expert who must attempt to explain to your audience the utility of computers, starting with how to turn the computer on to selecting which software program they want to use. In fact, you may even have to explain what software is. It is essential to use language that your audience can understand and revise your knowledge into terms that the "average" person can identify. You can then follow the guidelines we provided for descriptive speaking. This type of speech can be used for creative, thought-provoking topics as well as complex subjects. Examples of topics that might lend themselves to explanatory speaking are those that explain impressionist painting, tweeting, nuclear medicine, or our national debt.

Definitional Speeches

Definitional speeches are about concepts, theories, and philosophies. Most often, these sorts of speeches are about abstract topics. Therefore the purpose of a definitional speech is to convey information that will show your audience how the topic is relevant to their lives. Providing real-life examples and applications of the subject matter is essential. Examples should be explicit and clear.

Let's use the topic of politics to explore the characteristics of this type of speech. Your authors are aware, from their students, that a majority of them find politics to be an abstract concept. And while they have opinions about political issues, they typically don't understand how politics relates to their own lives. This is the type of subject that works well as a definitional speech. You would need to explain, or define the issue, and then apply that definition to an area of their life so that they can understand how the issue affects them personally.

Applying the Nine-Step Process for an Informative Speech

It is important to remember that all informative speeches are designed to give your audience real knowledge about your topic. Being exposed to a topic in an informative speech means that your audience will be taught new information about and understand your subject more clearly. Your speech should be factual, and personal opinions should not be included, although personal experience based on fact can add interest. Now let's follow the nine essential steps to an effective speech and you'll be on the right track to creating an effective informative speech.

STEP 1: CHOOSE YOUR TOPIC

First, pick a general topic. Refer to *Unit 2: What* and choose a general topic and then narrow it using the three-step narrowing process.

STEP 2: FOCUS YOUR TOPIC

As we have learned, you need to focus your topic for the audience, the occasion, and the speaking environment. Let's explore the steps in this process as they now apply to an informative speech and develop a working plan for our speech.

Audience: Element One

1. What do your audience members already know about your topic? This will help you decide how much research you need to do on your topic and whether your speech will concentrate on basics or more advanced information.

2. Where did your audience get its information? Is the audience's information credible? Is it biased? Is what they know based on their opinion or is it based in fact. This helps you decide on whether your main points will be clarifying what is true or provide other insight, such as how to apply the information you are sharing.

Occasion: Element Two

Knowing why you and your audience are gathering will help you set the direction your speech should take and is the second element of your working plan. Refer to *Unit 3: Who* if necessary.

Speaking Environment: Element Three

The environment you will be speaking in consists of the facility and general area in which you will address your audience. Refer to *Unit 3: Who* if necessary.

Now that you have found out detailed information about who your audience members are and have created a working plan, you should now be able to state what the audience will know when you complete delivery of your speech.

STEP 3: CONSIDER YOUR SPECIFIC PURPOSE

The general purpose of a speech to inform is to provide the audience with new information. Preparing a clear, concise statement that reflects the audience's response to your speech also helps you develop an informative speech that doesn't become persuasive. My audience will know the different blood types. This is a correctly written specific purpose for an informative speech. My audience will donate blood, is persuasive and therefore not appropriate. Frequently referring back to your specific purpose will help you develop a speech that stays focused on relaying *information*.

STEP 4: ORGANIZE YOUR SPEECH

It may help your speech be more effectively organized if you take another look at the categories of topics for informative speeches introduced earlier in this chapter. Speeches about objects need to be concisely organized because you can't present every detail about the object. Speeches about processes need to show step by step instructions from the beginning to the end of the process. These speeches also need clear visual presentation in the speech. Speeches about events need to be organized so that their relevance between the audience and current events is clear, even if the event is a past or future one. Speech topics that involve concepts need to include definitions of the main elements related to the concept early in the speech, either in the introduction or as your first main point in the body of your speech.

Additionally, when organizing your speech to inform there are three things to keep in mind.

1. Use simple logic.
2. Use repetition.
3. Use minimal, but important details.

You want to organize your speech from grabber to leaver in a user-friendly order. Avoid complex ideas and concepts that cannot be quickly understood. The logical flow of the speech should be apparent to you and your audience.

We learn by having something repeated to us over and over again. We endured hours of multiplication tables and flash cards, and endless lectures from our parents on the same topics for years. What links all those experiences together is that they were repetitive, and repetition is how we learn. In order for an informative speech to be effective it should include redundancy. That's not difficult to do when you realize the three parts of a speech are designed to be redundant. In the introduction of your speech, you tell the audience what you will tell them in your speech. In the body of the speech you actually tell them the information, and in the conclusion you remind them of what you just told them. Make sure that you organize your informative speech so that the main message is included in all three parts of your speech.

STEP 5: RESEARCH YOUR TOPIC

One question we often hear from our students is, "If I've picked something I know a lot about, why do I have to research it?" We say because an informative speech is a speech that does not include personal opinion, but does include personal experience supported by facts. Therefore you must research your topic no matter how much you believe you already know.

An informative speech builds credibility through information that is objective and based on fact. Researching your topic to verify that your information is credible is necessary. You should use a wide variety of sources (magazines, professional journals, interviews with experts, etc.) to get a balanced view of your topic. Citing your sources in the body of your speech adds to the credibility of what you say and makes it more likely that your audience will continue to listen to your speech. Research smart! Start with what you know, move on to find out what experts say and then try to find any additional information you may need (like videos, charts, audio clips, etc.). Once you have this framework, the next step is to "jazz it up."

STEP 6: CREATE PRESENTATION AIDS

Many people learn new material when it is presented to them in a visual manner, others when they can hear the information and, some people learn by doing. These various ways people learn are usually referred to as a person's learning style, how a person most easily learns new information. It is not however, the only way a person can learn. Most people learn well through visualization, no matter what their primary learning style. Therefore, giving the audience a visual representation of your topic will reach most of your audience. Use attention-getting elements in creative ways in order to help you reach your specific purpose of providing information.

STEP 7: CREATE SPEECH NOTES

The purpose of speech notes when you are delivering your speech is to keep you organized and spur your memory as to what "comes next." Notes for an informative speech should be easy to see so that you can remember several pieces of information with a glance. Speaking from an outline allows you to mark transitions and/or citations between points. However, direct quotes can be written out completely so you don't misquote.

STEP 8: PRACTICE

Practicing your informative speech several times greatly enhances the actual delivery. Practice your informative speech until it sounds logical and flows smoothly. Without practice you'll decrease your credibility and lose your audience. Practice aloud with a friend or family member who is unfamiliar with the subject you will be explaining. That way they can help you find spots in your speech that might confuse or lose an audience.

STEP 9: DELIVER YOUR SPEECH

You have done as much as you can do to prepare for delivering your speech. Believe that you will deliver the best speech you can and then do so. Keep your audience interested and use simple language. When we learn something new we do so through repetition, clear details, and examples. With proper organization that leads your audience to achieve your specific purpose, you'll deliver an informative speech that is not only successful but should result in a great grade.

Now that you have applied the nine-step process to prepare an effective informative speech, it is time to put it into action again to create a persuasive speech.

Situations Requiring Persuasion

This type of speech attempts to produce some behavioral response or attitude change in your audience. **Persuasive speeches** require the speaker to be thorough and convincing in order to get the audience to accept his or her viewpoint.

Many people view *persuasion* as the action of a salesperson or con artist. Yet, persuasion is actually an art that requires tremendous skill and, when done ethically, can be a significant factor in positive change. This type of speech requires getting your audience to think like you by providing them with sound reasons as to why they should accept your point of view.

Categories of Persuasive Speeches

Persuasive speeches can be categorized in three ways: speeches to stimulate, convince, or activate your audience. Let's look at each category in detail.

Speeches to Stimulate

A **speech to stimulate** is the easiest of the persuasive speeches because it attempts to strengthen beliefs already held by your audience. The stimulation speech resembles a pep talk. Think of a coach's speech to the team at half-time. If she does her job effectively, the team returns to the game with a renewed sense of direction and an attitude that can strengthen its resolve to win the game. Charities often use this method to get you to donate money. Since many people already believe it is "better to give than to receive," the goal becomes one of getting you to actually make the donation.

Speeches to Convince

These types of speeches are used to change the audience's mind. This speech attempts to convert the listeners' current way of thinking or behaving to what the speaker is proposing. An example of a **speech to convince** might be to ask the university to use funds that have been allocated for renovating the gym for building a student parking lot instead. It is important to note that you might not change their minds completely in just one speech. You are implying future action, but "today" you are trying to at least achieve a mental shift.

Speeches to Activate

This type of speech is used to get your audience to do something. You will ask your audience to take action during your speech. A **speech to activate** should change behavior. This type of persuasion challenges the audience's normal mode of behavior and offers them an alternative choice. You provide them information that establishes the need for change. For example, a local restaurant now has heart-smart menus because customers convinced the restaurant's managers that there was a need for healthier menu choices. These customers not only addressed the problem that these foods were not offered they made suggestions for specific items that could be offered and how to prepare them. This tactic persuaded the restaurant to take action and actually add the items to the menu.

Applying the Nine-Step Process for a Persuasive Speech

Persuasion attempts to change attitudes, beliefs, or actions through the use of information, but it can be challenging. However, with the proper preparation and organization, you will feel the exhilaration that comes from convincing a room full of people to support you and your ideas. Now let's get started and use the nine-step process to create a persuasive speech.

STEP 1: CHOOSE YOUR TOPIC

First, pick a general topic. Refer to *Unit 2: What* and choose a general topic and then narrow it using the three-step narrowing process.

While it is always important when choosing a topic for a speech to pick something you are interested in, it is essential for a persuasive speech. In the real world (outside the classroom) the reason you will be presenting a persuasive speech is because you feel passionately about some subject!

- Pick something you care about—so you can be enthusiastic about it.

- Keep it personal or local—topics that are "close" to your audience are the best choice. Don't try to persuade them to solve world hunger. Instead get them to fill a local food pantry's shelves as a step in the right direction.

- Keep it simple—Make sure the topic you choose isn't so complex that your entire speech is devoted to explaining what the topic is. All speeches need to have information, but remember you aren't giving an *informative* speech.

Take some time to consider how you feel about your topic. Once you are clear about how you personally feel about your topic, your belief then becomes a proposition, a statement that expresses an opinion or belief. In persuasive speaking there are three types of propositions. Each proposition accomplishes a different goal.

1. *A proposition of fact argues truth.* For example, making the statement that, according to history, a lone assassin shot President John F. Kennedy is a **proposition of fact**. The desired goal of such a proposition is to persuade the audience to accept your view of the information based on the facts you present.

2. *A proposition of value argues beliefs or judgments: right or wrong, moral or immoral, good or bad.* For example, making the statement that unions undermine the American work ethic is a proposition of value. The desired goal of such a proposition is to persuade the audience to agree with your judgment based on the facts you present.

3. *A proposition of policy argues that something should or shouldn't be done.* It involves both fact and value but goes a step farther by calling for a change in procedure. For example, saying grades should be abolished in college and a system of pass/fail instituted instead is a proposition of policy. The desired goal of such a proposition is to persuade the audience to agree with your decision on what should happen based on the facts you present.

STEP 2: FOCUS YOUR TOPIC

Now that you have a speech topic and a clear proposition formulated based on your personal belief about that topic, you need to focus your topic for the audience, the occasion, and the speaking environment. Let's explore the steps in this process as they now apply to a persuasive speech and develop a working plan for our speech.

Audience: Element One

Your audience analysis for a persuasive speech must be more detailed than for any other type of speech. In most persuasive speaking situations the audience will be a combination of those who already agree with you, those who disagree, and those who are undecided or apathetic about the topic. You should concentrate your focus on those who make up the largest percentage of your audience. However, you can't ignore the remaining listeners. You must always keep in mind the entire audience and their ideas and feelings, as this becomes the basis for the body of your speech.

If you are going to be effective in getting them to do what you want, you'll need to be empathic and "put yourself in their shoes." This requires learning as much as you can in your audience analysis about why they aren't already "in your camp." You'll need to find out what their objections are and address them in your speech. The better you understand your audience the easier it will be to get them to arrive at the conclusion you want. Always remember that persuasion is about them, not you. You must present convincing **evidence** to sway your audience to your viewpoint. Your audience will be committed to their own beliefs and be resistant to yours—at least initially. Find out as much about your audience and their beliefs as possible. Ask direct questions pertaining to your specific topic and their beliefs. In addition to the information you may already possess about your audience, it is a good idea to find out this added information:

1. *What do your audience members already know about your topic?*   This is useful to know when deciding whether to bring up arguments against your position. If they don't know about an argument, don't add fuel to the fire by discussing it. If they do, you'll have to make a defense.

2. *Where did your audience get their information?*   Is their information credible? Is it biased? How will you approach negating the source? Be direct when their source is factual, directly refute their position with new facts. Be more subtle when their information came from a source that stirred up an emotional response. An offended audience is an unreceptive one.

3. ***What is your audience's position on your topic?*** You need to
know your audience's thoughts and opinions. You need to know the
intensity of their convictions. It's one thing if I believe littering is
wrong. It's a much stronger level of involvement if I spend every Saturday helping to pick up trash littering local streets. Knowing the
strength of their opinions will help you direct the development of
your speech.

4. ***Why doesn't your audience already agree with you or why
aren't they currently doing what you want them to do?*** If you
don't discover these factors, you won't be able to persuade them at
all. You may have done your research and feel that you have all the
support for your topic that you need. But if your arguments don't
"negate" their reasons for not agreeing with or doing what you
want, you won't convince them. So if you are trying to get them
to exercise four days a week for 20 minutes a day, you will need
to know why they already aren't doing so. Those reasons *must be
disputed* if your speech for persuasion is to be successful.

Once you understand the audience's beliefs and opinions, in order to
persuade your audience to adopt your viewpoint, there are three additional
elements you must address. Historically in the study of communication,
they are known as *ethos* (credibility), *pathos* (emotion), and *logos* (logic).

1. ***Credibility—"ethos."*** One of the most basic elements of persuasion is that people aren't likely to change their views or actions
unless the person who is trying to persuade them is someone they
consider knowledgeable and trustworthy. Establishing this in your
persuasive speech is essential to effective persuasion. You'll need to
establish credibility in your introduction and build on it throughout the body of your speech by providing facts that are supported
with credible sources. This is known as making an appeal to ethos.

2. ***Emotion—"pathos."*** The second basic element of persuasion
deals with emotions. We aren't likely to change our view or actions
unless we believe the change will "make things better," thus establishing a need for change in the first place. Achieving change will require
you to appeal to the audience's feelings about your topic and use this
insight in your persuasive speech. This is known as making an emotional appeal.

3. *Logic—"logos."*   To persuade an audience you must also appeal to their sense of **logic.** While **emotional appeals** target our heart, logical appeals target our head. Providing rational reasons for change is important. Logical appeals require facts and figures to support the premise that is being presented, thereby helping your audience create an orderly succession of evidence that leads to an understandable conclusion.

In order to persuade audience members that your position is the one they should adopt or believe, you must consider their **needs** and desires in the initial stages of your speech. Then appeal directly to those needs using one or a combination of the appeals listed above. Studies show that emotional appeals are very effective in the short term, yet logical appeals have more long-term results. Therefore, a persuasive speech that grabs audience members by their hearts and then gives them facts to consider over time will optimize your results.

Once you have completed your fact gathering, you must apply these facts to help you focus your speech. By going through this process, you have prepared for the first element in your working plan, *the audience.*

Occasion: Element Two

Knowing why you and your audience are gathering will help you set the direction your speech should take and is the second element of your working plan. Refer to *Unit 3: Who* if necessary.

Speaking Environment: Element Three

The environment you will be speaking in consists of the facility and general area in which you will address your audience. Refer to *Unit 3: Who* if necessary.

Now that we have found out detailed information about who our audience members are and have created a working plan, you should now be able to state what the audience will know when you complete delivery of your speech.

STEP 3: CONSIDER YOUR SPECIFIC PURPOSE

Since your audience will be a combination of those who agree, those who disagree, and those who are undecided about your topic, when developing your specific purpose, focus the wording to reflect the majority of your audience. Make sure that your specific purpose clearly expresses your desired outcome. Is your purpose to get them to agree with your belief? Or is the ultimate outcome an action you want them to take? Start your specific purpose with a positive ultimate goal. The audience *will agree* that the president of the US should be elected by popular vote. The audience *will sign* a petition to allow cell phone use in school. Both of these examples demonstrate a clear and direct outcome that is persuasive in nature.

STEP 4: ORGANIZE YOUR SPEECH

Due to the complex nature of persuasion, the organization of your speech will play a significant part in its effectiveness. While a persuasive speech has an introduction, body and conclusion as any speech does, we have some special suggestions for organizing these speech elements.

Motivated Sequence

Monroe's Motivated Sequence is a five-step organizational pattern originally used for sales that was developed by Alan Monroe in the 1930s. Due to its psychological approach, this organizational method is extremely effective when an immediate change is desired and can be an effective tool for organizing a persuasive speech:

1. *Attention.*   Get your audience members' attention (grabber) and let them know your subject (preview). Prove to the audience that there is a problem, and answer the question "what's in it for me?" (WIFM). The best way to show WIFM to those you are trying to persuade is to immediately demonstrate it. Don't just tell them what they will gain from accepting your contention; provide them with an example to illustrate it (credibility). All of this takes place in your introduction.

2. *Need.*   Prove to the audience that they need to fix the problem. This is initially stated in your introduction (preview) but is developed and supported in the first main point of the body of your speech. Do this by telling them incidents that demonstrate such need and use as many additional facts, examples, quotations, etc., as required to make that need convincing. Establish the importance of the need for change for this audience.

3. *Satisfaction.*   Solve the now-established problem (need) by providing a feasible solution. This occurs in the body of your speech as your second main point. At this point you need to clearly establish the belief, attitude, or action you want the audience to adopt for your

topic. Make sure they understand what you are proposing and how the solution adequately and logically meets their need. This is where you will address the reasons your audience isn't already doing what you want them to and give them other options.

4. ***Visualization.***   Get the members of your audience to *see* how much better they will *feel* if they adopt your plan, or how bad they will *feel* if they don't. This follows the satisfaction step and occurs as the third main point in the body of your speech. The conditions you describe must be realistic. The more vividly you describe the situation the more persuasive you will be. An effective approach to accomplishing this is to explain one of the following, but not both:

   • ***The Positive.***   Describe your solution so your audience can actually picture the positive results of such a change in view or action.

   • ***The Negative.***   Describe conditions to show them how bad and unpleasant their lives will be if they fail to carry out your plan.

5. ***Action.***   This is what you want your audience to do. You can develop this step as the final main point in the body of your speech, but it works best in your conclusion as a *call to action*, a single statement that specifically asks your audience to do something. In your conclusion you will provide a summary of your main points (review); and then state the specific action or change you want the audience to make (call to action). Leave the audience with your own personal intent to pursue the action or belief you recommend (leaver).

Propositional Organization

   • In addition to following the motivated sequence method above, you can organize the body of your speech according to which type of proposition you have adopted relevant to your topic.

   • **Propositions of fact** can be organized so that each main point provides a reason as to why the audience should agree with you.

   • **Propositions of value** need to justify why your judgment is based on logical reasoning. You must define what that reasoning is and then explain why your arguments address those issues.

- **Propositions of policy** must establish the need for change. This can be accomplished using one of the following organizational patterns.

  - *Problem-solution order.* The first main point shows the need for a new policy while the second provides the plan for change. Your final point addresses why it is practical. The same is true for those policy propositions that argue no need for change. Initially you will explain why the policy should remain the same, and then show that a new policy would not solve any problems, and finally may even create more serious ones.

  - *Problem-cause-solution order.* These speeches will have three main points. The first will establish the existence of a problem, the second will analyze the cause, and the third will present and support the solution. While this organization is similar to the previous order, it can only be used effectively if your audience analysis indicates that the majority of your audience agrees your topic is a real problem.

  - *Comparative advantage order.* If the audience is already "leaning" in your direction and just needs a slight "push" to agree with you, you will find this organization the most efficient and effective. An audience that already believes that there is a need for change doesn't need a speech that spends a great deal of time saying change is needed. Spend the bulk of your speech on making each main point address why your solution is best compared to other solutions.

No matter which organizational method you choose, never have more than three to five main points in your speech. Note that the organizational patterns we provide adhere to this rule. Keep it simple; base your arguments on what your audience believes and contradict them with evidence that works to change their perception.

So much research has been done on how to persuade others that it's impossible to cover everything. However, the following theories will provide you with an idea of some of the techniques that can be incorporated into your speech and used to your advantage as you organize the body of your persuasive speech.

- **Reinforcement theory** can be used to convince audience members to believe you or do what you want them to do by pointing out the benefit gained by adopting your viewpoint. Conversely, pointing out the negative effects can show them the consequences of not adopting your stance. This method works well when you have chosen motivated sequence as your organizational pattern.

- **Modeling theory** uses the premise that our opinions and ideas are modeled on the views and actions of others, particularly those we respect. People observe and then model that which is important to them. This works well when comparative advantage order is used as the organizational pattern in your speech.

- **Cognitive dissonance theory** is based on observations that there is a conscious or cognitive tendency for human beings to decrease dissonance, an uncomfortable feeling caused by holding two contradictory beliefs simultaneously, in their lives. This dissonance can be decreased by changing one's attitudes or behaviors so that they are not in conflict with one another. Show your listeners how believing as they do is inconsistent with other beliefs they hold dear. This causes dissonance, which creates the need to restore consistency. Used correctly, this can be a powerful persuasive technique and can be used effectively with all of the organizational patterns we have presented.

- **Fear** is another technique that you may utilize. Human beings are sometimes motivated by the fear of consequences if they don't do what is asked of them. How often have you studied for an exam because you feared getting a bad grade? In the workplace, not doing your job can result in fear of being fired or demoted. The use of fear can be very effective as a persuasion tool if used ethically. Your appeal to the audience's *fear factor* must be factually based and you must provide a way for your audience members to decrease their fear by applying your offered solution. This method is especially effective when you are using the organizational pattern of problem-cause-solution.

STEP 5: RESEARCH YOUR TOPIC

Now that you have a basic organizational structure to guide your research and have a technique in mind for attempting to persuade your audience throughout your speech, get to work! Finding appropriate credible support for your arguments is a critical factor in how well you will persuade your audience. You will need relevant, authoritative sources to support your claims. This means you will have to do more research for a persuasive speech than for an informative speech, and your research should focus on ethics.

Ethics, or honesty, in public speaking is important, but especially so in persuasion. Ethical speakers are knowledgeable about their topic, convey accurate information, use sound reasoning, and avoid biased information. Ethical speakers do not infringe on the rights of others, and they treat audience members with respect. These characteristics are essential when thinking about how to prepare a persuasive speech.

Each major point in your speech should be supported with a variety of evidence. If you can't clearly support each point, you'll need to eliminate that point. For each potential source use the ABCD checklist from *Unit 4: How* and be sure your sources and reasoning flow in a logical manner. In addition, the following lists will help you determine logical support from illogical support for a persuasive speech.

Logical Support: Use These Types of Support

1. *Statistics.* Use percentages, fractions, or other numbers to support your claim. Keep statistics simple. "Last year 91,612 women were in state or federal prisons—which equals 6.6% of all prison inmates."

2. *Narratives.* Relate a documented or historical event. "Long ago, when dinosaurs roamed the earth . . ."

3. *Anecdotes.* Relate a "personal" story. "I volunteered at the annual 5k run." Showing your audience that you have personal experience with your topic is an excellent way to establish credibility.

4. *Analogy.* If two things are alike in some aspects, they may be alike in others. "Christopher Columbus navigated uncharted waters, so, too, our astronauts rocket into the unknown, outer space." While analogies are excellent sources, be sure to check that they are not comparing two very different things.

5. *Testimony.* Use expert opinion. Make sure you accurately quote or paraphrase statements. Be sure to explain to your audience the credentials the person has that make him or her an expert.

6. **Sensory evidence.**   Use examples that relate to one of the five senses. "We need to stop polluting the air in our neighborhood. Our children shouldn't breathe air that smells like rotten eggs." Permeating the environment with that odor would be even more dramatic and persuasive.

Illogical Support: Avoid These Types of Support

1. **Dicto simpliciter.**   Generalization. "Sugar is a source of energy; therefore, the more sugar I eat, the more energy I have."

2. **Hasty generalization.**   Too few instances to support a conclusion. "You can't sell your car; I can't sell my car. Therefore, no private owners can sell their cars."

3. **Post hoc.**   Cause-effect relationship is untrue. This happens when we leap from a simple brief relationship to a causal link with insufficient support. "Let's not take Joe with us; every time we take him we get a flat tire." If he goes, something bad will happen!

4. **Correlation vs. causation.**   Implying that just because there is a similarity in data one item must have caused the other. "Every year the amount of ice cream eaten in the US increases, as does the number of heart attacks. Therefore, ice cream causes heart attacks."

5. **Contradictory premise.**   Premise #1 contradicts premise #2. "[#1] If God can do anything, [#2] can He make a stone so heavy He cannot lift it?"

6. **Ad misericordiam.**   Appealing to sympathy. "I had to work overtime yesterday so you should give me extra time to complete my homework."

7. **False analogy.**   A comparison of two very different things. "The college shouldn't be able to dictate what classes I have to take to earn my degree; after all, the local supermarket doesn't tell me what groceries I can buy.

8. **Hypothesis.**   A statement that assumes fact. "If Mitt Romney had won the election in 2012, the unemployment rate would be lower."

9. **Stereotypes.**   Implying that what is true about one person applies to everyone in that race, gender, age, political party, etc. "All teenagers are poor drivers."

10. *Poisoning the well.* Slander or personal attack in an argument. "My opponent has lied. Therefore, you'll never be able to believe anything he says."

11. *Loaded question.* Implies an affirmative situation through a question. "Are you still cheating on your taxes? There is no good way to answer this type of question.

12. *Either/or question.* Two extreme choices. "We can continue this administration's policies that have bankrupted America, or we can elect a fiscally responsible government by electing Candidate Z."

13. *Slippery slope.* Arguing that one change inevitably will lead to another. "If universal background checks for gun purchases are mandated, the government will be able to take away your guns.

Once you have determined organization and logical support, you are now ready to enhance your persuasive speech by adding in your presentation aids.

STEP 6: CREATE PRESENTATION AIDS

Presentation aids used in your persuasive speech can be used to illustrate emotional appeals (showing a mangled car from an accident where the driver was texting while driving) or help the audience understand information presented in a factual appeal (showing a chart that lists statistics). The old adage "A picture is worth a thousand words" is particularly true in persuasion.

STEP 7: CREATE SPEECH NOTES

Since organization is so important in persuasion, using your outline as your speech notes is most effective. This will help you deliver your speech in a clear, understandable manner that will make it easy for your listeners to follow. In order to be ethical, you'll want to list all quotations as well as your sources on your outline to make sure you are correctly stating and orally citing them.

STEP 8: PRACTICE

Practicing your speech helps you to focus on the verbal and nonverbal delivery of your speech. Practice in front of a small group of people. Encourage them to give you feedback so you can adjust your speech accordingly.

Enthusiasm in your verbal and nonverbal delivery creates enthusiasm in your audience, which can result in the desired persuasive outcome. If you have followed our suggestions in this chapter you, too, can be an expert at persuasion!

Now that you have applied the nine-step process to prepare an effective informative speech and an effective persuasive speech, it is time to put it into action to create a special occasion speech.

Situations Regarding Celebration

The type of speech most people will present in their lifetime is the **special occasion speech.** These types of speeches typically mark special events, and speeches are often a major focus of these occasions. These speeches require you to work at placing audience members at ease so they can enjoy themselves at the event. Special occasion speeches are usually very short. Humor may be used, but a speaker need not be a comic to entertain an audience. Our culture abounds with events each year; therefore, you will likely be asked to give a special occasion speech at some point in your life. It is the most frequently delivered speech because eulogies, wedding toasts, introductions, anniversaries, and birthdays are frequent and common occurrences in our society. Rural areas, small towns, and cities alike all host a variety of events that include speeches delivered for specific events. Chances are, learning skills to use when giving special occasion speeches will come in handy several times in your life.

Categories of Special Occasion Speeches

There are as many different kinds of special occasion speeches as there are events. It would be impossible to provide a definitive list of all these speeches. Instead we've provided you with some information about the kinds of special occasion speeches most people will encounter. We have divided special occasion speeches into categories, grouping them by similarities, but be aware that many speeches share characteristics across several categories.

Awards

Awards are given to honor people at many events. There is usually someone who gives both a presentation and an acceptance speech. The main purpose of these events is to bring attention to quality and award those who characterize such a quality. These events usually include the word "award" in their title: Athletic *Awards* Banquet, Annual Outstanding Honors *Award*, Academy *Awards*, etc.

The purpose for giving a **presentation speech** is to give an award (or a prize, gift, or commendation) to another person. You should be brief and to the point, emphasizing the award itself and the person receiving it. You should discuss the history of the award and the reason that it is given. You should then point out the accomplishments of the award recipient and why he or she has been designated to receive the award. Do not overdo and do not under do. Be brief, precise, and to the point.

An **acceptance speech** is given in response to receiving an award. The purpose of this type of speech is to give honest and brief thanks for the award you have received. You should thank those who helped you to attain the award, but be brief and humble. There is no need to boast about your accomplishments; this would have been taken care of by the speaker who gave the speech of presentation.

Nomination

A **nomination speech** should stress characteristics that make the person being nominated the logical choice. Mention only his or her outstanding achievements and stress skills that make the nominee the most qualified person for the position. After all, you want the audience to endorse your nominee! Depending on the organization, you may be required to use a traditional manner of placing a name into nomination like, "I rise to place Julie Doe as our nominee for president of this organization." As a member of that organization you will probably be aware of this procedure if it is used, but it's worth investigating to make sure you correctly enter the nomination. Remember that you will probably be speaking to others who support your candidate so your main purpose is to get them fired up and ready to campaign or vote for your nominee.

Beginnings and Endings

Speeches to welcome, introduce, or bid farewell/celebrate retirement attempt to make a connection between an event and person. These types of speeches are usually one of many speeches given at the same event.

A **welcome speech** is designed to introduce your audience to a specific event. It is important to let the people you are welcoming know as much information as possible about the situation and the people present. You should be brief and honest. Make a statement about your hopes that the event will be beneficial for everyone and invite them to enjoy it.

An **introduction speech** is designed to create a connection between someone who is about to speak and the audience present at the event. These speeches should briefly tell the audience about the speaker, not disclose the speaker's complete biography! This is easily accomplished by talking in advance with the speaker or reviewing his or her resume. Use information that the audience will find interesting, significant, or appealing. It is important to pronounce the speaker's name correctly and stay brief. Stay within your time limit and present only information that is relevant, such as the reason the audience is there and the purpose of the upcoming speaker. *You* are not in the spotlight; that position is reserved for the speaker you are introducing. Don't talk about yourself or your ideas.

Farewell/retirement speeches are usually given by both the retiree and others present at the event. If you are presenting a speech to honor the person who is going to leave, don't try to tell everything about the person's life. Instead stress his or her outstanding accomplishments and positive influence on others. While it is fine to express that the person will be missed, don't focus on the leaving! Include the retiree's plans for the future and remind the audience that this is just the next step in his or her busy life. If a gift is being presented (as is often the case), give it at the end of the speech. Doing so makes a natural transition from you as the speaker to the retiree who will most likely give a speech of acceptance after receiving the gift.

When you are the one saying farewell the first thing you should do is thank those who have honored you at the event. You may also want to thank others who were significant in helping you achieve your goals. If your experience has been positive, that's not difficult to do; however, if you are leaving a negative situation, you may be tempted to use this speech as a way to vent. Avoid the temptation to talk about people who have wronged you, people who were mean, or those you believe stood in your way of success. Make your farewell a celebration.

Entertainment

In this category of toasts, roasts, and generally entertaining speeches, the speaker is usually expected to entertain an audience prior to some other event occurring or before a series of speeches. The purpose of the gathering will often determine the content of your **entertainment speech.**

Entertaining speeches given after a meal are often referred to as "after dinner" speeches. A speech to entertain probably requires more creativity and imagination than most other speeches. While the purpose of the event will determine the speech content, it is the speaker's responsibility to make a speech interesting and keep the audience's attention. Audience enjoyment is the desired outcome of such speeches. While we are entertained in many ways that are not necessarily humorous, one of the characteristics of entertaining speeches *is* the use of humor. For example, if you are gathered to celebrate someone at her 50th birthday party, your speech might be about the humorous elements of aging. You aren't expected to make the audience roll in the aisles with laughter. You are not expected to be Chris Rock or Sarah Silverman.

Many cultures, including our own, employ a tradition of honoring someone or something through the use of a **toast.** Some of the ones you are most likely familiar with are those presented at weddings by the best man or maid of honor. They can be humorous or serious depending on the situation or speaker. Toasts should be short, personal, sincere, and probably no longer than three minutes in length. Because of the nature of a toast, the use of note cards is usually unnecessary and may, if used, convey insincerity to your audience.

A **roast** may seem like a speech that attacks the guest of honor, but it is really a speech that uses sarcasm and comedy to honor a friend. Everyone has a different reaction to being the focus of sarcastic comedy. Before deciding to roast someone you'll need to make sure he or she has a sense of humor and can take criticism. If you decide to do a roast, you will usually focus on the person's "negative qualities" by pointing them out in a fun way. Don't use hurtful comments and stay away from behaviors or mistakes the person has made that you know he or she is sensitive about. Always conclude your speech with a positive comment about the guest of honor. Even though a roast makes fun of the person in a negative and sarcastic way, the audience should be left with the belief that you sincerely like and respect the honoree.

Special Events

July 4th and Martin Luther King Jr. Day are examples of past events in the United States in which a celebration speech may be given to show the extent of influence these events or people have on the present.

Commemorative speeches are ones that celebrate past events or current events that are tied to the past in some way. For example a birthday is a current celebration that is tied to a birth which occurred a year ago or more in history. Personal celebrations like birthdays and anniversaries tend to include family experiences and personal reflections. The most important factor for such speeches is to focus on points relevant to the event of the person's life you are celebrating. Do not attempt to make the speech a comprehensive timeline. These speeches should be brief, factual and sincere.

A **tribute speech** should point out the qualities and achievements that a person has attained in his or her lifetime. Tributes can be used in many situations such as funerals, birthdays, retirements, weddings, commencements, and keynote addresses. Sometimes a tribute uses humor, but the main goal of this type of speech is to effectively present information about a person's life. Remember to strive for sincerity, no matter what the occasion, while sharing as many details as possible about the honoree. It is helpful to include a statement about what audience members may have gained from knowing the person to whom the tribute is addressed.

Commence means to begin, therefore **commencement speeches** should focus on the dedication and hard work graduates have achieved to reach this point in their lives, while going forth to begin their future. Your authors, being academics who have attended a large number of commencements, have some tips for giving a commencement address. First and foremost, remember that the speech is not about you. While you can certainly include mention of personal experiences similar to those of the graduates, you need to focus on *the graduate*. Your grabber for these speeches is vitally important as the graduate is often preoccupied thinking about what will happen after the graduation, so you have to get his or her attention right up front so your words won't fall on "deaf ears"! Keep the speech under 20 minutes in length. Your speech is only one event the graduates will be experiencing that night.

Eulogies are given at a funeral shortly after the death of the person. However some may be presented at memorials held at a later date. While the general purpose is to honor the deceased, remember that you are giving the speech for the living, not the dead. Stress positive traits and achievements and emphasize the influence the person had on the people in attendance. A short biographical summary of the person is usually included in such speeches. The goal of a eulogy is to remind the audience that the event is intended to celebrate the life of the deceased, not the person's death.

Dedication speeches are given to honor the people and organizations that were instrumental in raising funds for or constructing buildings, monuments, artworks, and places. Typically these types of speeches begin by referring to why the group has gathered. They give a brief history of the object being dedicated and express thanks for anyone important in making it happen. Often the speech of dedication ends with the introduction of a person who is representing those who are being honored so they can accept the praise being shared.

While **inspirational speeches** are often confused with persuasive speeches to stimulate, they aren't persuasive because they are given to audiences who already agree with your viewpoint and are usually given during a celebration. This type of special occasion speech has the purpose of "rallying the troops" and is used to stir up emotion.

Unlike persuasive speeches, these **motivational speeches** don't need to include proof that what you are saying is true since the focus is on emotion not fact. However you do want to provide reasons they should be excited about the topic as well as inform the audience of specific behaviors they can take part in. These speeches include the familiar "pep talk" given by coaches prior to sporting events, speeches designed as sermons, and in general any speech whose main purpose is to increase emotional responses to a person, topic, or cause.

The main purpose of any special occasion speech is to make a clear connection between the unique reason for the occasion and the speech you are giving. Humor is generally appropriate and appreciated and is often a major characteristic of many special occasion speeches. You are typically provided with advance information that will help you to prepare your speech. You are often informed about your audience because you may know them personally or because everyone in attendance is there for the same reason. This makes special occasion speeches easier to prepare and deliver than informative or persuasive speeches.

Applying the Nine-Step Process for a Special Occasion Speech

Now let's get started and use the nine-step process to create a special occasion speech.

STEP 1: CHOOSE YOUR TOPIC

First, pick a general topic. Refer to *Unit 2: What* and choose a general topic and then narrow it using the three-step narrowing process.

Ask yourself the following questions when trying to decide on a topic for your special occasion speech:

- What's the purpose of the event?
- Why were you asked to speak?

Asking the purpose of the event will quickly guide you toward your general topic. Is it a celebration? Weddings, anniversaries, birthdays and a host of other events make picking your topic easy. If it's your grandparents' 50th wedding anniversary, you immediately know your topic is about them and/or longevity in marriage. Asking why you were asked to speak helps you find the topic as well. Being asked to speak at your grandparents' 50th wedding anniversary is probably due to your relationship with them. Are you the youngest, oldest, or only grandchild? Did you spend vacations at the lake with them? Whatever your special relationship is should help you find the topic on which you'll want to speak.

STEP 2: FOCUSING YOUR TOPIC

Audience: Element One

A special occasion speech, like all speeches, must be focused for the audience, the occasion, and the environment. While focusing for the audience is important, in a special occasion speech the likelihood is you won't have to spend a lot of time (as you do with other types of speeches) finding out the audience's knowledge, interest, and purpose. The reason for this is probably obvious; you most likely already know these people. Giving a toast at a wedding or providing a eulogy means you know the people you will be speaking to, making audience analysis quick and easy.

Occasion: Element Two

Knowing why you and your audience are gathering will help you set the direction your speech should take and is the second element of your working plan. Refer to *Unit 3: Who* if necessary.

Speaking Environment: Element Three

The environment you will be speaking in consists of the facility and general area in which you will address your audience. Refer to *Unit 3: Who* if necessary.

- What is the physical environment? Special occasion speeches often include using a microphone. Learning how to use it and, if possible, practicing with it before speaking is very useful in an effective delivery. Focusing for the environment of a special occasion speech probably includes a "dress code." Showing up in casual wear when others are dressed in black tie won't put you or your audience at ease.

- What is the time factor? It is important to be aware of the time limit of your speech. With rare exception, special occasion speeches should be relatively short. In many occasions you may be one of many who will be speaking. These events may also have other activities on the agenda (dinner, business meeting, dancing, etc.). You'll want to be aware of all the activities on the agenda when you speak.

STEP 3: CONSIDER YOUR SPECIFIC PURPOSE

Our students often ask if they "have to develop a specific purpose for this speech?" The answer is yes; every speech that is effective has a specific purpose. If you don't know what you want to accomplish, you won't be successful. The main thing to remember about special occasion speeches is to remember your purpose in giving the speech. While these types of speeches may inform or persuade, that is rarely their main purpose. Instead of "The audience will know my grandfather's life story," "The audience will know why my grandfather was special to me" is more appropriate and reminds the audience of the reason for the event.

STEP 4: ORGANIZE YOUR SPEECH

Because special occasion speeches are typically short, beginning public speakers often believe that organizing this type of speech in outline form isn't important. Nothing could be further from the truth. In fact, if you are to stay within your time limit you will need to have an outline so your speech will flow in a logical manner. Refer to the brief explanations for each type of speech. This will give you an idea as to what should be covered in the speech, and hence you will have your main points.

STEP 5: RESEARCH YOUR TOPIC

Since the majority of special occasion speeches will include personal reflection, you may find that you don't have to do much research. However, it is still important that any information you give is correct, so some research may be necessary to verify names, dates, or other details. Personal interviews are often the best form of research to fill in details about someone's personal life.

STEP 6: CREATE PRESENTATION AIDS

As with any speech, presentation aids help your audience understand your topic and add interest. However, if your speech is less than five minutes in length, incorporating a presentation aid may not be feasible or, perhaps, even necessary. In addition, the physical environment in which you will be speaking may not provide the means for incorporating some types of aids. For example: If you are giving a wedding toast in an outdoor venue where there is no projector system, you couldn't show a slide show or picture montage. Check for any equipment that is available in advance and adjust presentation aids accordingly. Remember, these events are often about people, and the people themselves can serve as their own visual aid!

STEP 7: CREATE SPEECH NOTES

While having notes to help you deliver your speech is always helpful, special occasions may hamper your ability to use them effectively. Once again, the length of the speech and the physical environment are factors in deciding if you want to prepare notes for your speech. Since many special occasion speeches are not necessarily presented formally "behind the podium," you may not have anywhere to place your notes. If you have a microphone in one hand and a note card in the other hand, gesturing will be limited. If you have to lay your notes on a table, they may be too far away to read them easily. We suggest that you create speech notes for special occasion speeches to practice with no matter what the length of the speech. However, if your speech is less than five minutes and you have no way of using notes effectively during your delivery, then don't.

STEP 8: PRACTICE YOUR SPEECH

Since special occasion speeches are typically short, involve topics you have personal knowledge of, and are given to an audience you may be familiar with, there may be a tendency to think that it isn't necessary to practice. You may decide that instead of presenting the speech in the extemporaneous manner we have learned, you can simply "think on your feet" and present the speech impromptu. This approach will usually result in an ineffective delivery with unconnected ideas and time fillers, not a smooth flowing speech the audience can easily follow. Finally, if you don't practice, you won't be able to time your speech, and you'll run the risk of throwing off the entire agenda of the event. Practice, practice, and then, practice some more.

STEP 9: DELIVER YOUR SPEECH

The big night has arrived, and if you have followed the nine essential steps of the speech process, you're ready. Take a deep breath—now go celebrate!

Conclusion

In this unit we have taken a look at how the nine-step process is applied to a speech. We have examined the three categories of speeches: informative, persuasive, and special occasion and applied the process in each instance to create a podium-ready speech. This process is an effective technique that will result in an organized speech every time it is used!

■ **DISCUSSION QUESTIONS**

1. How often in a day do you think you hear and give informative speeches?

2. What strategies can you use to make sure your informative speech does not become persuasive?

3. What are some areas in your life where skills in persuasion would be an asset to you?

4. When persuading, why is it essential that you address those areas where your audience disagrees with you?

5. Why are logical and emotional appeals both necessary in an effective persuasive speech?

6. What types of special occasion speeches have you given or anticipate giving?

7. Do you believe that special occasion speeches are easier to prepare and deliver than other types of speeches? Why or why not?

■ KEY WORDS

acceptance speech
cognitive dissonance theory
commemorative speech
commencement speech
dedication speech
definitional speech
demonstration speech
descriptive speech
emotional appeals
entertainment speech
ethics
eulogy
evidence
explanatory speech
farewell/retirement speech
fear
informative speech
inspirational speech
introduction speech
logic

modeling theory
Monroe's Motivated Sequence
motivational speech
needs
nomination speech
persuasive speech
presentation speech
propositions of fact
propositions of policy
propositions of value
reinforcement theory
roast
special occasion speech
speech to activate
speech to convince
speech to stimulate
toast
tribute speech
welcome speech

While

. . . continuing to apply the nine-step speech process . . .
. . . while delivering a group presentation . . .

- The Basics
- The Decision-Making Process
- Group Roles
- Accomplishing a Specific Task
- Handling a Crisis
- Working Online

Now that we have prepared an informative, persuasive, and special occasion speech, the final instance of where you might need to prepare and deliver a speech is while you are a functioning member of some type of group. We will now apply the nine-step process to preparing a group presentation.

Group Presentations

Throughout this text, we have prepared you for speaking as an individual to a collective group of people, your audience. However, some of your future speaking will involve speaking collectively with others as a member of a group. This process is known as **small group communication** and occurs frequently in modern-day society. It is estimated that twenty million meetings occur every day. These meetings occur in thousands of locations, for just as many reasons, throughout the world. The Internet has made global communication easy, and research shows that executives may spend two-thirds of their day in some type of meeting, whether in the boardroom or online. Effective small group collaboration skills are mentioned by CEOs as one of the skills recent college graduates often lack. If you want to be hired or promoted, the likelihood is that your own small group communication skills will be a major factor in those decisions.

While we tend to think of groups as formal entities associated with work, school, or organizations, we all belong to many "informal" groups. We are continually involved in small group communication with our family and friends. Since we so frequently are expected to work within groups, we need to understand how groups function before we learn how to present a group speech. All groups share similar characteristics no matter what environment they meet in or what their stated task or goal.

Although our society was founded on beliefs that the interests of individuals should take precedence over those of the state (a doctrine of **individualism**), it does utilize **collectivism** throughout its structure. When individuals live in a group, whether it is a family, a local community, or a country, the needs of the group will in some instances supersede those of each individual. Thus, our society is a blend of collectivism and individualism. Most religious and educational institutions, corporations, and governmental agencies use some form of collective group structure to accomplish their work. Maybe you are part of a crew at McDonalds or sing in a choir. Do you head a Spanish club, or are you a member of Future Business Leaders of America? Individuals in groups share information and make choices. Most groups form to accomplish a particular task, such as developing new procedures for fire drills, voting on whether to purchase new computers, or planning a local fund-raiser each year. Other groups meet for the purpose of social interaction and enrichment. Examples of these types of groups include Bible study groups, book clubs, and support groups. Although groups are formed for various reasons and to accomplish different tasks, the process for success is the same. As a reasoning member of a society that uses group process, you should be aware of how an effective group functions and be able to work within one, as well as learn how to prepare a speech to address or report the group's goals or tasks. The next time you are asked to report the success of your sorority's annual fund-raiser or present your book club's list of readings, you will be able to do so effectively.

The Basics

There are three basic elements that contribute to the success or failure of any group in accomplishing its goal. These elements include group composition, group size, and group time restraints. In order for a group to be effective these elements should be addressed.

1. Group composition

    - All group members must act cohesively and work toward a common goal.

    - All group members must seek and share information.

    - All group members must be flexible and adapt to the ideas adopted by the group.

    - All group members must share responsibility and support the group.

2. Group size

    - A group must include at least three people.

    - Odd-numbered groups are more efficient.

    - Groups of five or seven appear to function best.

3. Group time restraints

    - Meeting time depends on the type of group and its purpose.

    - **Primary groups** such as family and friends exist for the long term.

    - **Secondary groups** are formed to accomplish a specific task and exist for shorter periods.

    - There is no minimum or maximum time frame for a group to be effective.

    - A group will continue to exist until it decides its task is complete.

There are many advantages to working in groups. On the whole, people usually enjoy the interaction that occurs when working with other people since human beings, are for the most part, social creatures. According to most psychological studies, social interaction is one of the basic components of human need. Participating in a group gives us a chance to make our views known and share them with others. This form of interaction provides us with a rewarding experience. It makes us feel good to be a functioning member of a successful group. That is why working with others in a group is usually more socially rewarding than working alone.

In order for all group members to get along, it is often necessary to be cognizant of others and place our own needs and desires on hold. Remember that group members must be willing to let go of individual ideas and adopt those of the group. In a group, the concept of **synergy** applies—the combination of the parts working together has more value than each individual part working alone. You might think of synergy as 1 + 1 = 3! When people come together and share their experiences and knowledge, wonderful things can and do happen. Individuals working alone often make biased judgments and decisions that can lead to inappropriate actions. Individuals often see only their own viewpoint and not the whole picture. In a group, the influence of the other group members can help individuals maintain an open mind and stay focused on the larger issue.

One of the factors in reaching a decision in a group is the quality and quantity of information collected. Five people can collect and remember five times the amount of knowledge that one can. Group members may trigger or cue new information from one another, thus leading to more information being shared. Group decisions are usually more accurate than individual decisions. You have probably heard the saying, "two heads are better than one"; that's exactly what this means. When people form a group, they individually contribute their research, opinions and ideas. They can then collectively examine all of these ideas about an issue in depth and come to a decision more effectively than one person alone.

Working in a group will take more time than working on your own. One person usually can arrive at a decision in less time than it takes a group. This characteristic can easily be confirmed the next time you and your friends are trying to decide where to eat dinner or what movie to see! In a group, not only must each person come to an individual decision, all members must then share their decisions to collectively reach a final decision. Individuals may be influenced and motivated by others' behaviors, their environment, or their own physical or mental state. All of these individual motives and factors must be addressed during the group process, and this takes more time. In addition, since each group member comes to the process with their own knowledge, opinions, and ideas, some people will carry individual agendas into the group process, which can result in the group failing to achieve its goals. When a group needs to make a decision there are four methods the group can use:

1. **Majority rule.** This process requires the group to come to a decision by voting. If 51 percent or more of voters favor an issue or idea, then majority rules. If there are diverse opinions or loyalties in a group, these conflicts can be solved by using this method.

2. **Consensus.** This method occurs when all members of the group unanimously agree on an issue. A consensus is usually arrived at through a series of discussions. No vote is necessary as everyone will eventually hold the same thought or idea. Decisions arrived at through the method of consensus are usually the most effective. However, consensus is time-consuming, even when opinions don't differ greatly, and vastly time consuming when they do!

3. **Popular vote.** This method is similar to majority rule. The major difference in a popular vote is that the issue adopted by the group is the one that receives the most "popular" votes. For example, if there are 12 members in a group and four vote for idea number 1, five vote for idea number 2, and the remaining three members vote for idea number 3, then idea number 2 wins by "popular" vote. In other words, the most members voted for this issue. In fact, in this particular example, only 42 percent of the vote won the decision. If time is running out and discussions have failed to solve an issue, a popular vote may be required.

4. **Compromise.** If none of the other methods work, members can reach a decision through compromise. In this method some members forego their opinions in favor of what works for the group as a whole. While this method of decision making is perhaps the most commonly used, it should be noted that it may not be the *best* choice.

Whether you call it cooperation or **cohesiveness,** group members must stick together and work for the common good of the group. This means that at some point, the group must choose a course of action appropriate for the overall task at hand. Effective groups consist of people who work *together*, with members sharing equally in the responsibilities of the group. This cooperation fosters empathy and shared understanding, which in turn leads to better communication, increased productivity, higher morale, and group loyalty. This feeling of "oneness" with the group is probably the single most important factor in effective group interaction.

A significant part of group process involves the individual roles members will adopt within the group. The primary role that we usually think about when discussing small groups is who will assume the role of leader. However, there are many other roles you need to understand as well. These include task roles, maintenance roles, and personal roles. Understanding these roles can help you to make your group more efficient and cohesive. Let's begin with the **leadership role.**

Leadership Role

The first question that comes to mind in a group is, "Who's in charge?" If the group is organized for a goal other than mere social interaction, who will get things going? Although your professor or boss may not have assigned a group **leader,** one will nevertheless emerge. In a group, several personality types will be present, and one will usually dominate. This person will become the driving force for the group, or the leader. In fact, even when a leader is assigned, the real leader of the group may not be the person who actually has the label. It could be someone else!

What is this person like? What are the attributes of a good leader?

- A leader is confident, open-minded, generous of spirit, and courteous.
- A leader helps the group focus on its goal and get started in the right direction.
- A leader molds the individual members into a cohesive group by drawing out members of the group to learn what their opinions are on an issue. It may require drawing out less talkative members and reigning in those who try to monopolize the discussion.
- A leader should summarize major decisions made to keep the group on track and move the group toward the goals established.
- An effective leader facilitates tasks of the group; but does not assume responsibility for doing everything. An effective leader is one that others will follow because they want to, not because they believe they have to.

While typically a leader will emerge (whether one is appointed or not), it is possible that a group may be leaderless. Although this does not often occur, if it does, it is usually the result of one of the following factors:

- Two or more group members are competing for the role of leader and the group splits in loyalty. This can make the group environment tense and ineffective.

- All members of the group assume responsibility and take turns filling the leadership role. This can facilitate group process and still result in the group accomplishing its goal.

If the leader of the group is not functioning properly, what can be done? Change leaders! Your group is a democratic organization and, as such, is governed by the same rules. You have learned four ways to make a decision in a group. Use one of these decision-making processes to replace your leader. When enough of the group members feel that a change at the top is in order, that change should take place. Remember, you are functioning as a group, not as individuals, and the group's goal is more important than any one individual's search for self-gratification. With the proper leadership, your group stands a good chance of reaching the goal you set with a minimum of hassles.

Just as the leader has a role to play, so do the other members of the group. We are sure you will be able to recognize your friends, and perhaps yourself, in these various small group roles.

Task Roles

Roles that emerge due to the task-oriented nature of the group are called **task roles.** These roles help group members organize the work of the group to accomplish its goal. There are many task roles that are directly linked to a specific job. The following is a list of some of the most common task roles and their function/definition:

1. The *recorder* keeps track of the group's progress by taking notes, recording facts and figures, or keeping track of members who are present or absent.

2. The *opinionator* expresses his or her opinions and beliefs freely and without hesitation.

3. The *initiator* gets the ball rolling by proposing new ideas or different procedures.

4. The *clarifier* makes sure other group members understand problems and ideas by paraphrasing information to make it clear.

5. The *informer* is loaded with a wealth of information, providing facts and statistics relevant to the group's task.

6. The *coordinator* arranges details such as seating, room arrangement, and equipment necessary to complete the task. This person makes copies or brings a laptop or tablet for looking up information or recording notes.

7. The *energizer* is just like the bunny! This person keeps going and going and going, and makes other group members go too!

8. The *inquirer* makes requests for short but detailed information by asking questions, seeking opinions, and looking for facts. This person keeps the group focused.

9. The *evaluator* reminds the group of standards they have set and measures suggestions against such standards.

10. The *tracker* shifts the group's discussions and attention back on task when things have gone off track.

In groups where task roles are shared equitably, satisfaction with the group process is high. There is increased cohesion among members and a successful group outcome is the usual result.

Maintenance Roles

Group cohesion develops in such a way that **maintenance roles** also evolve; these roles are necessary for the overall good of the group and allow the group to interact in a smooth and supportive way. Maintenance roles keep the group working harmoniously. Where task roles are necessary to achieve a desired outcome or goal, maintenance roles are necessary to create a harmonious environment in which group members can be happy and productive while working to achieve their desired outcome or goal. The following is a list of some maintenance roles that may be assumed by members of the group:

1. The *stress buster* functions much like a medieval court jester. Just as the jester kept the king happy and in a good mood, this person uses humor to keep the group in a good mood.

2. The *harmonizer* does not sing; rather, this person helps group members settle conflicts and acts as an overall mediator between group members.

3. The *gatekeeper* controls the flow of communication, often opening the door for members to contribute new ideas. Sometimes, this function requires closing the door. This person may ask members to share ideas, while at the same time keeping others from dominating discussions. Controlling both elements is necessary for the group to function smoothly.

4. The *cheerleader* does just that—encourages other members to contribute and lets them know their ideas are valuable and appreciated.

5. The *collaborator* is one who connects the dots and points out similarities in group members' ideas in order to make mutually agreeable decisions and solutions easier.

6. The *parent* is friendly and shows care and concern for group members. This person will ask a group member about how something went, or ask how members are feeling each time the group meets. This is the member who often provides refreshments!

Assumption of maintenance roles is as essential to effective group process as the leadership role and task roles. They are the "heart" of the group process. They keep the group functioning by providing emotional encouragement to the individuals who make up the group.

Personal Roles

Thus far we have discussed roles that greatly aid the group and its members to achieve the overall goals set for the group. Unfortunately, since groups are composed of human beings, **personal roles** will also emerge based on individual personalities. Personal roles generally bring frustration to group work. The selfish characteristics of some people, and their disregard for the larger good of the group, can cause chaos for other group members. These saboteurs can seriously impair productivity and even be responsible for the group not meeting its goals. The following is a list of personal, self-centered roles and the dysfunction they can cause:

- A *freeloader* is any group member who does not participate in the group process. Freeloaders do not make individual contributions, and their lack of collaboration is frustrating. Freeloaders typically do very little, if anything, to assist the group in achieving its goal but expect to reap the benefits of the group's collective rewards.

- The cousin of the freeloader is the *do-it-all*. This is the person who takes control of the group and insists that everything be done his or her way. These people immediately make assignments to the rest of the group and typically write the report, or prepare the presentation, using their own ideas and research. They are not leaders and are not in real collaboration with the rest of the group. They focus only on themselves.

- The *monopolizer* is the person who consumes group time by taking too much time working in or assuming a role for which he or she is not suited, skilled, or prepared.

- The *joker*, unlike the stress buster (who uses humor to put other group members at ease), uses humor inappropriately to get laughs and to poke fun at and distract members from their work.

- The *antagonizer* is the thorn in everyone's side and promotes arguments and conflict with all group members.

- The *roadblock* has strong personal opinions and views and is unwilling to abandon these views for the good of the group. This creates an impasse that is difficult to maneuver around, much like *do not cross* signs at a real roadblock!

- The *self-seeker* always wants the attention of the group on him or her. This person may brag about past accomplishments or tell personal stories unrelated to the task at hand simply to keep members focused on and listening to him or her. It's all about meeeeeeeee!

- The *poor me*, like the self-seeker, shifts attention to him- or herself. However, the purpose in doing so is to get members' sympathy. Poor me's are the people who always have an excuse as to why they can't meet with the group or haven't been able to do what they were asked to do at the last meeting. They may use illness, working two jobs, being a single parent, or schoolwork to justify their lack of participation in the group.

Effective collaboration can be rewarding. Groups often find the best solutions to problems. However being an effective group member requires time and dedication to the group's goals. As Henry Ford said about teamwork, "Coming together is a beginning. Keeping together is progress.

Working together is success." Because solutions to a problem or the way to complete a task will not necessarily be evident, the group must discuss, evaluate, and weigh options to make the best decision for their topic and for their presentation if one is required.

Groups are usually created for one of three reasons: to accomplish a specific task, to handle a crisis, or to manage or resolve conflict.

1. **Specific task.** All members of the group collectively pursue a specific task, or common goal. **Committees** are formed to accomplish a specific purpose for a determined length of time. The word *committee* is often preceded with a term or phrase that indicates the committee's singular purpose, such as awards banquet committee, dance committee, or budget committee. Each of these committees meets until a predetermined deadline occurs, and the group is motivated to complete the task and report their findings.

2. **Crisis situation.** Group members gather to respond to a problem that needs immediate attention, often without advance warning. Generally they have some background knowledge or individual expertise related to the topic or task that requires a meeting. In a crisis situation, group members are required to assess a situation and make decisions based on limited information. Once the initial crisis is under control, problem-solving groups are formed to find a more long-term solution that can be implemented to remedy the identified problem. Citizen utility boards, fund-raising groups, and neighborhood watch groups are examples of problem-solving groups formed from crisis situations.

3. **Conflict management** or **conflict resolution.** Corporations are common environments for conflict management groups. Individuals or representatives of groups with conflicting interests or perspectives meet collectively to come up with strategies and techniques to manage the conflict so it doesn't escalate, or to resolve the conflict altogether, known as conflict resolution. Skills in bargaining and negotiating are important when trying to manage clashing personalities.

We find that most groups that are created fall into one of the categories listed above, and it is likely that most of us will need to function effectively within one or more of them during our school or business careers. Our research shows that corporations rate employee skills in communication and group process much higher than possession of a master's degree! These corporations believe that decisions reached in groups are more effective, and therefore more valuable, than those reached by individuals. Group work also abounds in civic, religious, and educational environments. Even family groups and groups of friends function more harmoniously when members interact well with one another. You will be part of many groups in your lifetime, so it is important to understand group process and realize that the end result of most groups will be a report of findings in the form of a presentation or speech.

Online Groups

In today's society group interaction often occurs in the online environment. Essentially every aspect previously discussed and explored is the same whether group communication is in a face-to-face or online environment. An effective group is an effective group, no matter the environment it is working within. There will still be need for leadership and collaboration. Effective task and maintenance roles will need to be filled. Personal roles may interfere. And there is no doubt that time will be required to achieve the group's goals effectively. There are, however, a few additional considerations when the group is going to be interacting via the Internet. Primarily these additional considerations will depend on whether the group will be communicating synchronously or asynchronously.

Synchronous communication takes place when two or more people are in contact with each other in real time, much like when we are speaking to each other in a face-to-face situation. Examples of synchronous communication forums include chat rooms and Skype as well as many others that allow for instantaneous communication. Groups using this type of communication differ very little from traditional group meetings that take place face to face. The major factors are deciding what software to use to allow everyone to chat, and when everyone can be logged in at the same time. This is essentially the same as a face-to-face group deciding on when and where the group will meet. However, a few additional considerations should be taken when participating in a synchronous online group:

- Using a synchronous function requires that everyone is familiar with the software and how it functions before the meeting takes place. If your group members all have Facebook accounts already, or are familiar with another common program, then that decision becomes easier.

- Be aware of time zones. If your group is composed of members from various time zones, make sure that everyone understands the exact time (in their zone) for the meeting. If the group consists of people in numerous time zones, some members will need to be willing to stay up very late or get up very early.

- Don't take too long. Synchronous sessions can significantly decrease the amount of time it takes to make collaborative decisions. If you take several days to arrive at a mutually agreeable time or spend several days planning only to find that there is no feasible meeting time for all group members, you've wasted, not gained, time.

With the exceptions mentioned above, live synchronous online meetings through the use of Internet technology function as effectively as their traditional face-to-face counterparts.

Asynchronous communication doesn't require all group members to be logged in at a set time. This approach uses software that functions much like the old bulletin board concept. Someone posts a text message early in the morning and a reply is posted and received at some later time or date. Online classes use forums for asynchronous discussion. These forums function much like when you post something on a friend's Facebook wall and the person responds by contacting you the next time he or she logs on or at some other convenient time. There is still collaboration, but it isn't instant. Because of that, when group communication is asynchronous, the following guidelines should be utilized to make it most effective.

- Login frequently to check for posts from other group members that need to be read and replied to. If all group members don't log in frequently it can take days to make decisions. Logging in every 24 hours or less makes it much more efficient for the group to proceed toward its goals. If you know you won't be logging in for more than 24 hours, let your group know and give them permission to make choices without you.

- Make posts significant. Since asynchronous collaboration usually requires more time than synchronous and face-to-face means, when making posts to your group's discussion make sure you advance the discussion toward consensus by making useful posts. For example when trying to make a specific group decision don't post, "What does everyone want to do?" Instead, post what you propose to do and your openness to share ideas and change your original position. Let your group know your strengths with PowerPoint, paintbrush, or other graphic software. This makes it quicker and easier for a group to make decisions.

• Avoid personal roles. While all personal roles should be avoided in any group, the asynchronous process becomes particularly ineffective when there are freeloaders or do-it-alls . When you aren't required to log in at a particular time, it's easy to become a freeloader, and when it takes more than a few hours to get replies, many people become do-it-alls to decrease their stress and possibly protect a grade.

What works and doesn't work in online groups is much the same as in a face-to-face group. Online groups can be very effective if each group member is dedicated to spending the time and effort needed to collaborate toward the final goal.

A working knowledge of group process will help everyone be a more effective group member. This should result in successful group collaboration and a rewarding experience for all.

Applying the Nine-Step Process for Group Speeches and Presentations

Once groups have accomplished their task or goal, many must present their findings in a collaborative speech or presentation. Although these presentations can be structured similarly to speeches for a special occasion, to convey information, or to persuade, group speeches have some elements that make preparing for and delivering them unique. Not all small groups will include a formal presentation as a goal. However, when they do, preparing a group speech will follow the same process as preparing an individual presentation. We will now apply the nine-step process to preparing a group speech.

Step 1: Choose Your Topic

First, pick a general topic. Refer to *Unit 2: What* and choose a general topic and then narrow it using the three-step narrowing process.

Frequently the general topic or subject of the group presentation will be assigned by those asking the group to meet and make a presentation. If your topic is supplied, the group simply moves to the next step, the focusing process. However there are times when the group, as a whole, must decide on a topic. Keep in mind that the topic chosen by the group must be one that all members share an interest in and no one is strongly opposed to. Otherwise those uninterested in the topic will quickly become nonproductive group members. The group must understand the problem to be solved or information to be conveyed (in the same way an individual speaker must understand the topic of his or her speech).

STEP 2: FOCUS YOUR TOPIC

Audience: Element One

All presentations will be more effective when the audience's interests, knowledge, and purpose are known and addressed. An audience analysis is always necessary for an effective interesting presentation.

Occasion: Element Two

Knowing why you and your audience are gathering will help you set the direction your speech should take and is the second element of your working plan. Refer to *Unit 3: Who* if necessary.

Speaking Environment: Element Three

The environment you will be speaking in consists of the facility and general area in which you will address your audience. Refer to *Unit 3: Who* if necessary. You must adequately plan for all members of the group. Who will speak, who will use what equipment, and who will keep your group minutes or notes.

STEP 3: CONSIDER YOUR SPECIFIC PURPOSE

Most groups will find that their general purpose is to either inform or persuade, so the wording of the group's specific purpose will follow the guidelines for all specific purposes and be worded according to the general purpose of the audience being informed or persuaded.

STEP 4: ORGANIZE

A group speech will need to include an introduction, body, and conclusion. There are four different styles of group presentations.

Unlike the way speeches are differentiated, by purpose, group presentation styles are categorized by the way in which the presentation takes place.

The most common type of group presentation is a **panel discussion.** They consist of a small number of people (typically 3–7 members) who are experts on a topic and a moderator who facilitates the discussion by maintaining an orderly flow of conversation and insures that all issues are covered. The moderator makes an introduction of the panel members and the issue being discussed as well as making a summative conclusion. If a question-and-answer period follows with the audience, the moderator directs that section of the presentation. Panel members are responsible for presenting various aspects of the topic and discussing among themselves the issues that the group has decided are most important. The interaction between members is not formally structured and the flow is more conversational. The purpose of a panel discussion can be either informative or persuasive.

A **forum** is similar to a panel discussion because the majority of time is devoted to questioning members of the group on the issue at hand. The moderator will provide an introduction of topic and members. Then each group member will give a very short overview of an important aspect of the topic (usually no more than three minutes). Once each member has given their opening remarks, the moderator will shift directly from the group to questions from the audience; this does not occur in a panel discussion. This style of presentation is typically used at conferences and seminars where the audience consists of people who are already knowledgeable about the topic so that questions asked are specific and require the members to verify and support the individual information presented. The purpose of forums can be either informative of persuasive.

A **symposium** is a series of short speeches presented by each member of the group focusing on a different aspect of the group's topic. It is more structured than a panel discussion and there is no discussion among the members during the presentation. Each member delivers a speech, uninterrupted by questions. The moderator's role is primarily the same as during a panel, including the facilitation of any question/answer period that may follow the formal presentations. The purpose of a symposium is to inform.

The fourth type of group presentation is a **debate.** This type of presentation is very structured with very specific rules. The group will be divided into two subgroups based on a proposition (EX. "The United States should abolish the Electoral College method of electing a President."). One group supports the proposition and the other opposes it. Depending on the wording of the proposition, one group will have the burden of proof while the other will attempt to negate their proof. The group who has the burden of proof will speak first followed by the other. This "back and forth" continues until the established parameters have been met. The group on whom proof resides has the last speaking spot. The purpose of a debate is persuasion, not of the opposing group, but of the audience. Note, a formal debate has very structured rules that go beyond what we have presented here. If you participate in a formal debate, be sure you learn and understand all the rules.

STEP 5: RESEARCH YOUR TOPIC

In order to avoid problems in a group, members must be able to gather and share information. This is the only way that valid decisions can be made no matter what decision-making method is used. The process of gathering information is best handled by group members individually researching and gathering information related to a specific part of the task. There is no need to duplicate efforts, so dividing up the research is a time-saving practice. However, all information gathered will need to be shared with the group as a whole so decisions can be made in a collaborative manner.

If group members fail do to research, or if only a few members do research, the session is apt to be a waste of time or will resemble a lecture period rather than a group work session. Group members should apply the ABCD method (see Unit 4: How) to check the credibility of their individual research choices prior to sharing them with the group as a whole.

STEP 6: CREATE PRESENTATION AIDS

As with any presentation, aids help explain pertinent information. Therefore the use of such aids should be an intricate part of the delivery. While individual members will probably be responsible for developing such aids, each aid should be discussed, agreed on, and shared with the group before being used during delivery of the speech.

STEP 7: CREATE SPEECH NOTES

For a group presentation each speaker will be creating his or her own notes, which will contain the data the person individually needs to share during the group delivery. Just like individually prepared presentation aids, notes must be shared in advance with the entire group. In addition to individual notes, group members should collaborate on and create a group outline or agenda that is shared with the audience as a "delivery guide" so that the transition from speaker to speaker and point to point will be clear and effective and more easily followed by the audience.

STEP 8: PRACTICE

While many groups will ignore this step in the process, they do so at the expense of the final presentation. A practice session will assure that the allotted time limit is met. It will also make sure individual presentations are of approximately equal length, verify that all pertinent information is delivered, and help the group transition smoothly from section to section within the presentation. Since group presentations are often followed by a question/answer period, creating a list of anticipated questions and practicing what the group answers will be is also advised.

STEP 9: DELIVER YOUR SPEECH

When the time arrives for the actual group presentation, the group will have devoted dozens of hours (individually and collectively) to preparing for what will typically be an hour or less of actual presentation time in front of an audience. Keep in mind that all group members will be seen by the audience even when they are not talking, so it's important to monitor the messages group members are sending during the presentation, whether they are speaking or not. Prior to delivery, group members should discuss what dress code should be adhered to, where members will sit or stand when not speaking, and how the audience will be addressed during the question/answer period.

Now that you have participated in a group and prepared a group presentation, you can use the following form to analyze the effectiveness of your group process, thereby adjusting any items prior to your next group collaboration.

Strengthen Your Skills

Group Analysis Form

Group Climate: Each of the statements below refers to a different aspect of group climate. In one of the five spaces at the right of each statement, place a check mark to indicate your best estimate of that aspect in your group.

Aspect of Group Climate	Outstanding	Superior	Average	Poor	Unsatisfactory
Pleasantness: Everyone seems to enjoy the group.					
Security: Members feel safe speaking.					
Cohesion: Members support one another.					
Purposefulness: Goals are understood.					
Objectivity: Members seek the best solutions to a problem.					
Involvement: Members are eager to participate.					
Cooperativeness: Members contribute to the best of their ability.					
Communication: Remarks are addressed to all; no cliques form.					
Permissiveness: Atmosphere is relaxed, and informal.					

(Continued)

Productivity:
  Members keep at
  the job and pro-
  duce effectively					

Integration:
  Group involves and
  utilizes all members,
  not just a few.					

Flexibility:
  Group adjusts to
  change and benefits
  from mistakes.					

Contributions: List the name of each participant in your group (include yourself) above a column (seven columns are provided below, but you may need less or more than that). Then in the appropriate box, indicate how often each member acted as indicated in the first column. Use the following scale to denote the frequency:

4 = Often

3 = Occasionally

2 = Seldom

1 = Never

	Name	Name	Name	Name	Name	Name	Name
Contributes							
Gives information							
Asks for information							
Gives opinions							
Defines, clarifies or shows relationships							
Asks for definitions or clarification							
Argues or refutes (supported)							
Argues or refutes (unsupported)							
Supports others, praises, defends							

(Continued)

Releases tension, jokes, shows satisfaction							
Shows tension, withdraws, blocks or attacks others							

Group Roles:

1. Who do you believe was the leader in your group? Why do you think so? Was this person an effective leader—why or why not?

2. What task roles were taken on by individual members of your group? Who did what?

3. What maintenance roles were taken on by individual members of your group? Who did what?

4. What personal roles emerged and in which members of your group? How did they affect the group as a whole?

Conclusion

In this unit we have taken a look at how the nine-step process can be applied to a group speech or presentation. There will be many instances in our lives when we will have to function as a member of a group, and ultimately report the findings of this group process. The nine-step process provides an effective means to achieving podium-ready group presentations.

■ DISCUSSION QUESTIONS

1. Name three groups of which you are a member and the roles you perform in each.
2. Discuss the advantages and disadvantages of working in a group.

■ KEY WORDS

asynchronous communication
cohesiveness
collectivism
committees
compromise
conflict management
conflict resolution
consensus
crisis situation
debate
forum
individualism
leadership role

maintenance roles
majority rule
panel discussion
personal roles
popular vote
primary groups
secondary groups
small group communication
specific task
symposium
synchronous communication
task roles

Final Thoughts

We started this text by stating that life is full of questions. Hopefully some of the questions that you had about public speaking have been answered. Now that you have had some of your concerns addressed, we hope you are beginning to feel more comfortable with the study of public speaking.

This text was divided into seven units. Each unit covered a basic universal question: why, what, who, how, when, where, and "while." We introduced you to a nine-step process that will help you prepare a speech from beginning to end no matter what type of speech you may be asked to prepare and deliver. We often take our communication for granted, not realizing how important communication is in our daily lives. Communicating with others on a daily basis requires the ability to exchange our thoughts, feelings, and ideas. To function effectively in society, you must be able to get your messages across to all kinds of people in many different situations. You are now equipped with the knowledge and skill to do so! Good luck at the podium!

Glossary

acceptance speech   Speech given in response to receiving an award.

adrenaline   A hormone produced by the body under stress resulting in a boost in energy.

antilistening behaviors   Behaviors that result when we give in to distractions and may occur if we have not had any formal training in listening, or when we are taught not to listen.

appearance   A nonverbal element that gives the audience an impression of you based on how you look.

articulation   The process of emitting clear, individual sounds that form distinct spoken words.

assumptions   The belief that we have heard the information before, that we know what the speaker will say, that the message is insignificant, or that the information is just not applicable to us.

asynchronous communication   A form of online group communication that takes place at different times and doesn't require all group members to be logged in at a set time.

attending   The second step in the listening process that consists of trying to pay attention to the sounds we hear.

audience analysis   The process that involves: (1) gathering demographics about your listeners—such as age, sex, and occupation, (2) analyzing listeners' psychological makeup, group memberships, etc., and (3) applying the data to ensure their interest in your speech.

audio clip   A recording that can enhance your speech when played for the audience.

authority   Refers to an author or information provider who is an individual and/or an organization, possessing experience and/or knowledge that qualifies him/her/it as a valid source of information.

bias   A political or ideological preference that is stated or implied.

bibliography   A list of sources in alphabetical order; there is a standard form for the information listed in the bibliography—often MLA or APA.

blackboard   A board on which you can make quick drawings or charts during your speech.

brainstorming   Collecting many ideas quickly as they occur to you, without analyzing each individually.

causal organization   Outline progression organized to show cause-and-effect relationships.

CEM   An acronym that stands for "control, eliminate, and mask"; a process that can help you control your anxiety, eliminate symptoms of it, and mask nervous behaviors during speaking.

channel   The medium through which a message travels to reach its audience.

chronological organization   Outline progression organized by time occurrence.

cognitive dissonance theory   Suggests that inconsistencies create discomfort or conflict, which then creates a need to restore consistency or comfort.

cohesiveness   The ability to function as a group and achieve the group's goals by putting aside individual gratification.

collectivism   A theory that promotes the idea that the needs of the group supersede those of each individual.

commemorative speech   Speech that celebrates past events or current events that are tied to the past in some way.

commencement speech   Speech focused on the dedication and hard work graduates have achieved to reach this point in their lives, while going forth to begin their future.

committees   Groups formed to accomplish a specific purpose for a determined amount of time, generally labeled according to the group's reason for meeting.

communication   A free exchange of thoughts, feelings, and ideas to ourselves and others.

communicator   A person involved in exchanging messages with one or more other people.

compromise   A decision where some members must abandon their opinions in favor of what works for the group as a whole.

conclusion   The last part of the speech, which summarizes your main points, links back to the introduction, and notifies the audience you are finished.

conflict management A form of group process widely used at the corporate level in which members meet collectively to bargain and negotiate final decisions on various issues.

conflict resolution Coming up with strategies to deal with conflicting interests or perspectives so a group can function effectively.

consensus Coming to a decision when all members of the group unanimously agree on an issue.

content The breadth and depth of the material supplied.

credibility An audience's perception of you as trustworthy based on your knowledge of the subject and your personal appearance; also the third part of the introduction.

crisis situation A form of group process in which group members are required to assess a situation and make decisions based on limited information.

currency The age of the information being used.

debate A type of group presentation that is structured according to very specific rules.

decoding Translating verbal and/or nonverbal symbols received into mental images.

dedication speech Speech given to honor the people and organizations that were instrumental in raising funds for or constructing buildings, monuments, artworks, and places.

definitional speech Speech that shows an audience how abstract topics are relevant to their lives.

delivery The process of presenting your information to an audience.

demographic data Measurable statistics such as age, income, and gender about audience members; used in audience analysis.

demonstration speech Informative speech that shows the steps necessary to take a process from beginning to end.

descriptive speech Informative speech that uses words to paint a clear picture of a person, place, or thing.

design The layout of a Web site.

diaphragm A muscle located under the rib cage, which determines lung capacity.

digital presentation Displaying information by using computers, software, and projectors.

emotional appeals Used in persuasive speeches to make a plea to the feelings of the audience.

encoding Translating mental images into symbols.

entertainment speech Speech that includes toasts and roasts and is generally given to entertain an audience prior to some other event occurring or before a series of speeches.

enunciation The act of pronouncing individual vowel and consonant sounds.

ethics A system that entails honesty, guiding speakers to convey accurate information.

eulogy Speech given at a funeral or memorial service after the death of a person.

evaluating The third step in the listening process where we attempt to understand what is being communicated to us and determine its familiarity and/or importance to us.

evidence Anything created and substantiated by another person that is not your personal opinion.

explanatory speech Informative speech that provides a clear explanation of a complex issue or idea.

extemporaneous delivery Giving a speech that is prepared and practiced from an outline or notes, not memorized or read from a manuscript.

external noise Distractions that occur outside the body and interfere with the listening process.

eye contact Directly meeting the audience's eyes with your own.

facial expressions Animation of the speaker's face that conveys to the audience how the speaker feels.

farewell/retirement speech Speech usually given by both the retiree and others present at the event.

fear A persuasive technique that uses the audience's apprehension to motivate them.

feedback The constant and simultaneous exchange of verbal and/or nonverbal messages between communicators.

fillers Ineffective words or sounds, such as "um" and "like," which weaken the speaker's delivery and causes the speaker to appear hesitant and unprepared.

fluidity The ease and smoothness of verbal delivery.

focus The process of narrowing your speech to reflect what effect it will have on the target audience.

formal outline A document that arranges material in an orderly and easy-to-follow format, according to certain rules; final outline often submitted.

forum   A group presentation, used at conferences and seminars when the audience is familiar with the topic.

general conversation   Any daily conversation occurrence that could produce a possible subject/topic for a speech.

general topic   The starting point of any speech; the theme or subject of a speech.

gestures   The movement of hand(s) or body to add emphasis to important points in the speech.

grabber   An interesting way of gaining the audience's attention, and the first part of the introduction.

grammar   The system of word structure and arrangement for language.

habits   Behaviors we engage in consistently without conscious thought.

handout   A copy of information related to or in your speech that you can give to each audience member.

hearing   The reverberation of sound waves in the ear.

hitchhiking   The process of building off of topics/subjects in a list to generate additional topics/subjects.

impromptu delivery   Giving a spontaneous, unprepared speech, usually given on the spur of the moment without any prior notice.

individualism   A theory that promotes the belief that the interests of individuals should take precedence over those of the state.

informative speech   A speech whose main purpose is to increase the audience's knowledge about a particular subject.

inspirational speech   Special occasion speech given to stir up emotion and "rally the troops."

internal noise   Distractions that occur inside the body that interfere with the listening process.

Internet   An intangible place where you can obtain information and communicate with people via computers; also known as the Net and the Web.

Internet address   A unique URL—uniform resource locator—that must be entered into a Web browser to access a specific Web site.

interview   A research method by which you question someone and record his or her answers.

intrapersonal communication   The communication inside your own head; the "voice" in your head. It can interfere with listening.

introduction   The first section of a speech that gains attention, connects the speaker to the audience, provides credibility of the speaker, and presents the topic.

introduction speech Speech designed to create a connection between someone who is about to speak and the audience present at the event.

language A written or spoken system of rule-governed symbols that are used to convey a message.

larynx Contains the membranes known as vocal chords; air passing over it provides sounds called tones.

leadership role The person who facilitates the achievements and tasks of the group, by inspiring trust, listening to others' ideas, and attempting to understand others' opinions.

listening The psychological process that requires an active willingness of a communicator to not only hear but also understand a speaker.

logic The orderly succession of evidence leading to an understandable conclusion. Reasoning that is rational and includes facts and figures.

maintenance roles Group roles that help achieve group cohesiveness.

majority rule Decision-making process that requires 51 percent or more of the group vote.

manuscript delivery A speech given by reading from a paper text or off a teleprompter.

media Methods of distributing or transmitting information— Radio, TV, newspapers, magazines, DVDs, CDs, the Internet.

memorized delivery Giving a speech that is recited from memory; an ineffective delivery style because sometimes the speaker forgets or repeats an item.

message An idea, thought, or emotion transmitted from one person to another.

message overload Excessive amounts of information that saturate our brains and cause us not to listen.

model A pictorial representation of an idea or concept.

modeling theory A theory that asserts that using examples that the audience views positively increases the probability of motivating your audience to model or accept your viewpoint.

Monroe's Motivated Sequence A five-step process created by Alan Monroe in the 1930s that can be used to organize an effective persuasive speech.

motivational speech Speech designed to increase emotional responses to a person, topic, or cause.

narrowing Honing a topic so it interests both the speaker and the audience and fits the purpose of the speech.

needs The physical and psychological factors that human beings rely on; desires that motivate choices in human beings and are the basis of a persuasive speech.

noise Physical or psychological barriers—internal or external—that interferes with the accurate sending or receiving of a message; distractions.

nomination speech Speech that stresses characteristics that make the person being suggested the logical choice.

nonverbal elements Elements of communication that are not language specific: such as eye contact, gestures, tone of voice, and so on.

object An item that is the exact, real one about which you are speaking.

occasion Event or purpose for which a speech is given.

organizational pattern Way of dividing and ordering your main points so that your speech will move from point to point in a logical and easily understood progression.

organize The act of deciding three to five main points and how they will be developed in your speech.

outlining Organizing and arranging your material in a way that is orderly and easy to follow.

panel discussion A group presentation consisting of several members who are experts on a topic and a moderator who facilitates the discussion.

pauses The time between sounds or words.

personal environment The total experience pattern, background, and value scheme from which a person thinks, acts, and speaks.

personal experience The knowledge you've accumulated during your lifetime, which can be a good starting point for a speech.

personal roles Those individualistic and self-centered roles that hinder a group's ability to achieve its task.

persuasive speech Speech that attempts to produce some change in attitude or behavior in an audience, and attempts to gain agreement from the audience to adopt the speaker's viewpoint.

physical needs Basic human needs that include food, clothing, and shelter.

picture A visual image that helps the audience understand your material by "seeing" it.

pitch Refers to range, or where a sound would be placed on a musical scale.

plagiarism The use of another person's work without giving credit to that person.

popular vote   Decision process that chooses the item that is the most popular with group members, not necessarily gaining the highest percentage of votes.

posture   The manner in which the speaker holds his or her body.

practice   Rehearsal of a speech.

preoccupied   Mentally absorbed with our own thoughts.

presentation aids   Elements that *show* the audience what you are describing, allow them to *hear* something, or in some other way help them *experience* your words. Examples include charts, graphs, pictures, Power-Points, and audio and video recordings.

presentation speech   Speech designed to to give an award (or a prize, gift, or commendation) to another person.

preview   The last step of the speech introduction—a statement that lists the main points of the speech.

primary groups   Groups that exist for the long term, such as family groups.

priority organization   Separates items by importance, least to most important or the reverse.

problem solution organization   Outline progression that poses a problem and then offers a solution.

process organization   Outline progression that organizes material according to a series of step-by-step actions.

pronunciation   Separating and accenting syllables in the correct manner.

proposition of fact   Persuasive argument that proposes that something is factual.

proposition of policy   Persuasive argument that proposes a course of action.

proposition of value   Persuasive argument that proposes that something is right or wrong.

psychological data   Measurable information about the morals, values, beliefs, and lifestyles of your audience members; used in audience analysis.

psychological needs   Needs stemming from our state of mind, including morals, values, and being a contributing member of society.

rate   The speed at which your words are delivered.

reinforcement theory   Theory that suggests that behavior can be changed by pointing out rewards or consequences of adopting a particular viewpoint.

research   The process of gathering information for your speech, which may include quotations, statistics, or examples; research supports your ideas and gives the audience the information they need to believe you.

research plan   Guideline for researching that addresses what information you need, why you need it, and where to find it.

responding   Final step in the listening process in which we send a speaker a message that indicates we have received his or her message; also known as feedback.

retaining   Step 4 in the listening process, which relies on memory to recall information.

roast   A speech using sarcasm and comedy to honor a friend.

secondary groups   Groups formed for a short period of time to complete a specific task.

semantics   The meaning of words.

sensory mode   Which sense we use to comprehend new information; often this mode is visual.

small group communication   Working collectively with others; communication within a group that consists of at least three people who interact for the purpose of attaining specific goals.

spatial organization   Outline progression that organizes material according to geographical space or area arrangement.

speaking environment   The third element of your working plan, consisting of the facility and general physical area in which you will address your audience.

speaking outline   The outline you take to the podium.

special occasion speech   A speech designed to keep the audience's attention and interest for a short period of time, usually connected to a special event.

specific purpose   Being clear about the end result of your speech.

specific purpose statement   A single sentence that states the response the speaker wishes the audience to have at the end of the speech.

specific task   A goal that is collectively pursued by a small group.

specific topic   The result of the focusing process; a narrowed or "specific" topic.

speech anxiety   The physical and psychological (often unfounded) apprehension or fear of speaking in public, including giving a speech.

speech notes   The notes the speaker actually takes to the podium; the notes you may adjust when you practice your speech.

speech process   The nine steps that incorporate and summarize the concepts, skills, and practices that make a speech effective.

speech to activate   Persuasive speech that asks the audience's participation in some action.

speech to convince   Persuasive speech that converts the audience to the speaker's viewpoint.

speech to stimulate   Persuasive speech that increases beliefs already held by the audience.

speech topic   An idea that interests you and that you can talk about.

stage fright   Opening-night jitters suffered by professional actors and sometimes experienced when speaking in public.

surveys   Instruments designed to gather factual data or opinions from people by asking questions about a specific topic.

symbol   A mental image.

symposium   A series of short speeches presented by each member of the group focusing on a different aspect of the group's topic.

synchronous communication   A form of online communication that takes place when two or more people are in contact with each other in real time.

synergy   The concept that the combination of the parts has more value than each part working alone; $1 + 1 = 3$.

task roles   Group roles that help the group organize and accomplish set goals.

toast   Speech that is short, personal, sincere, and no longer than three minutes in length.

tone   The combined vocal elements of rate, pitch, and volume.

transition   A word or phrase used within a speech to shift from one point to another, such as *however, for example,* and *in addition.*

tribute speech   Speech that highlights the qualities and achievements attained by a person in his or her lifetime.

verbal elements   Words and language used to represent images and ideas when delivering a message.

video   A visual aid that helps the audience understand your material by "seeing" it.

vocals   The sounds we make caused by breath.

voice   A combination of elements such as tone, rate, pitch, and volume that, depending on how you use them, affect the verbal delivery of your speech.

volume   The loudness or softness of the tones produced when sound resonates in your sinus cavities.

welcome speech   Speech that introduces the audience to a specific event or outcome.

whiteboard   A board on which you can make quick drawings or charts during your speech.

WIFM   An acronym that stands for "what's in it for me"; gives the audience a reason to listen to you; the second part of an introduction.

working outline   Organizational tool used by a speaker during the early speech preparation period to decide the most effective order for presentation.

working plan   Defines and incorporates your audience analysis with what you know about your occasion and speaking environment.

Index